To my wife

Betty

Preface

For too long now the church has neglected mentally retarded persons and their families. Even when pastors and laymen are moved to compassion by the needs of these persons, they are often frustrated simply because they do not know how to help. As a state hospital chaplain, I have observed both helplessness and unconcern by churches. I have also observed the isolating effect this has on those persons affected by mental retardation. My purpose, therefore, is to bring into sharp focus what I perceive to be the church's ministry in mental retardation.

So that this book might speak directly to pastors, Christian education directors, denominational workers, church school teachers, and interested professional persons, frequent use is made of actual experiences and case studies. With the exception of chapters 4 and 7, most of these materials are not my own. They represent what has taken place in local churches. I am indebted to several persons for sharing these materials: Clyde C. Bryan, Tom Boyd, J. E. Crane, Samuel Gerth, David R. Grant, Herschel Hobbs, Henry Marksberry, Wallace Morton, Wayne E. Oates, Samuel Southard, J. Harold Stephens, and Robert Wilson. More extensive case materials were made available by William Foote, Robert W. Mayes, Mrs. T. N. Scriptures, V. Roland Simpson, and A. Richard Smith. Parts of the manuscript were read by Miss Annie Ward Byrd, Baptist Sunday School Board, Miss Margaret Fernea, University of Tennessee School of Social Work, and Allen Greene, Clover Bottom Hospital and School.

Two influences are obvious in these pages. One is that of my former teachers of pastoral care: Wayne E. Oates and Samuel

Southard, Southern Baptist Theological Seminary, Louisville, Kentucky; and LeRoy Kerney, Edward Thornton, and Joseph W. Knowles, Institute of Religion, Texas Medical Center, Houston. Of particular help with this manuscript was Samuel Southard who read a "rough" first draft and offered many valuable suggestions. I publicly acknowledge my indebtedness to him. The other influence is that of the staff of the Clover Bottom Hospital and School who permitted me to function as a full member of the interdisciplinary team. Many of my insights into the "religion of the retarded" resulted from this collaboration.

My wife has been a co-worker in this ministry. Not only has she led the music for the Sunday morning worship service and participated in special worship experiences on Easter and Thanksgiving, she also supported my desire to write by giving up time that rightly belonged to her.

Finally, I can only partially acknowledge my appreciation to the fourteen hundred residents of the Clover Bottom Hospital and School. My insistence in these pages that mentally retarded persons are genuine human beings with religious concerns is the fruit of this sharing.

HAROLD W. STUBBLEFIELD

Contents

1

The Challenge
to the Church

Mental retardation is a problem involving almost every minister and church. A survey of 220 Protestant and Catholic clergymen revealed that 92 per cent had had previous contact with mentally retarded persons and their families and 62 per cent currently have parents of retarded persons in their churches. A majority of these ministers had performed a variety of services for both the retarded and their families.[1]

A growing awareness of the church's responsibility in mental retardation, however, is unaccompanied by certainty as to the nature of its role. For example, in a recent survey, one minister discounted the necessity of co-operating with other professional persons in rendering services to the parents of retarded persons. "Other help is needed," he said, "but the minister and church are of utmost importance." Some ministers, on the other hand, disavowed their responsibility by contending that only professionally trained persons should work with the retarded and their families or that the pastoral ministry consists only of referrals to community agencies. A pastor limited the extent of his responsibility to "mostly co-operation with agencies established for this purpose." Another clergyman stated that the church should offer help only "if asked" by the parents. Other ministers openly denied that the church has any responsibility in mental retardation. As one pastor remarked: "I think all are concerned over this situation. However, I do not believe it is the work of the church."

Ministers are not alone in their confusion. Lay workers engaged in the religious education of retarded persons in the local church often express impatience when asked to view this ministry in a

1

broad context. In a conference on the church and mental retardation, several participants did not want to spend conference time discussing the nature of mental retardation, the problems which retardation creates for the family and community, nor the church's motivation for such a ministry. They wanted only to secure materials and methods to use in their special classes at home.

When churches and ministers, however, attempt to develop a comprehensive ministry to the retarded and their families, they are frustrated by the absence of printed resources. For example, the educational board of a major denomination sought to stimulate churches to minister in this area by publishing articles in denominational magazines. When pastors and religious education directors responded to the challenge and requested specific help in the form of printed materials, none was available nor planned for the near future. Moreover, the numerous articles, pamphlets, and books published since 1946[2] give little specific assistance. They were designed largely to arouse the interest of the church by portraying the retarded as persons with needs similar to those of other persons and by suggesting areas of service for the church. With few exceptions, these writings have not grappled with the major issues nor have they presented demonstrations of effective ministries. Many of these writings are repetitious, drawing heavily on the field of special education and related disciplines or reporting personal observations and experiences without developing basic principles.

In essence, the present status of the church's involvement in mental retardation can be characterized like this. There is a growing recognition that the church has a definite ministry to the retarded and their families and that denominational and interdenominational educational agencies are responsible for producing resource materials to assist churches. Although not widely recognized, some pastors are presently rendering a ministry of pastoral care, and many churches are providing religious training for the retarded. However, the specific forms which the church's ministry should take are undefined because many areas of the problem have not been explored. Almost no writings are available which adequately describe the relation of theology to mental retardation, the pastoral care of the retarded and their families, or the religious development of the retarded. No acceptable religious education curriculum is presently available.

This pioneer ministry challenges the church to clarify its perspective. Clarification is most needed in three areas: the nature of mental retardation, the identity of the church in relation to mental retardation, and the nature of the church's ministry.

The Nature of Mental Retardation

Basic to the church's ministry is a correct understanding of mental retardation. An aggressive and enlightened ministry can only emerge from a right perspective toward the problem. The ministry of the church has been extremely handicapped by the superstition, folklore, and ignorance associated with mental retardation. At least four stereotypes and misconceptions need to be exposed.

The first stereotype is the tendency to view mental retardation as a moral problem. For instance, a clergyman visiting a state institution for retarded persons asked the superintendent if smoking and the use of alcoholic beverages by the mother during pregnancy were causes of mental retardation. A more extreme view is the belief that God causes mental retardation. This belief was evident in the remark of a church member: "Sometimes God gives a retarded child to punish us for a great sin." Similarly, another church member believed that a "mentally retarded child is a result of the will of the Lord. It is not to be questioned and dwelled upon."

These moral interpretations, the product of a prescientific era, are shattered by current scientific knowledge. The presently accepted definition of mental retardation by the American Association on Mental Deficiency is: "Mental retardation refers to subaverage general intellectual functioning which originates during the developmental period and is associated with impairment in adaptive behavior."[3] Impairment must be present in at least one of the following areas of adaptive behavior: (1) maturation, (2) learning, and (3) social adjustment. The rate of maturation refers to the rate of development of self-help and other motor-sensory skills of infancy and childhood. Delay in acquiring these skills is important as a criterion of detecting mental retardation during the preschool years. Learning difficulties are usually most apparent after the child has started to school and is important as a qualifying condition of mental retardation during school years. Social adjustment is important as a qualifying condition of retardation during adulthood. This refers to the person's ability to maintain himself independently in the community through gainful employment.

Mental retardation has two basic causes: biological and environmental. The biological cause has to do with "those factors which produce anatomical or chemical abnormalities of the nervous system and thus interfere with the ability of the brain to respond normally to environmental stimuli."[4] Retardation due to brain pathology may be caused by infection, intoxication, trauma or physical agent, disorder of metabolism, growth, or nutrition, new growths, prenatal influence, or by an undetermined cause. This cause of retardation is prevalent in all social classes.

The environmental or psychological cause refers to "cultural and environmental factors which, through the establishment of unhealthy or inadequate patterns of intellectual response, may prevent the optimum functioning of the mind in a person whose nervous system is basically capable of normal activity."[5] Retardation with psychological causes is subgrouped into three categories: mental retardation associated with environmental deprivation, mental retardation associated with emotional disturbance, and mental retardation associated with psychotic disorder. Retardation due to environmental deprivation occurs in the lower socioeconomic classes of society, while retardation associated with emotional disturbances or psychotic disorder may occur in any social class.

A second stereotype is the identification of mental retardation with other disabling conditions. Frequently, mental retardation, mental illness, and other handicapping conditions are not separated. In distinguishing between mental retardation and other disorders two criteria are used—intellectual and social. The double criteria is necessary, because, as Heber says, "it is the impairment in social adaptation which calls attention to the individual and determines the need for social and legal action on his behalf as a mentally retarded person; it is the below-average intellectual functioning which distinguishes mental retardation from other disorders of human efficiency."[6]

In addition to distinguishing the retarded from the mentally ill, a distinction is also necessary between the retarded and other "exceptional" persons. Although the general classification of "exceptional" persons is helpful in identifying those persons who cannot benefit from education designed for "average" persons, "exceptional" persons do not comprise a homogeneous group. For example, both the gifted and the retarded are classed as "exceptional" persons, even though they are at opposite ends of the intelligence continuum. Since the unique feature of mental retardation is the subaverage intellectual functioning, the educational and psychological problems are different from those in deafness, blindness, emotional distur- bance, and other handicapping conditions. Mental retardation is a distinct and separate social and educational problem.

A third stereotype is that mentally retarded persons themselves comprise a homogeneous group. One pastor, for instance, mistakenly assumed that all retarded persons were so severely retarded that a pastoral ministry to them was impossible. He said that ministering to the retarded is "like ministering to those in hospitals who may not be conscious; one goes and prays and indicates an interest." Simi- larly, special religious education classes in churches are sometimes organized without regard to the retarded's different levels of mental ability.

Identification of the different levels of retardation is the key to an effective religious ministry. For educational purposes, the re- tarded are grouped into three categories: nursing care, "trainable," and "educable." Of the total number of mentally retarded persons, it is estimated that 85 per cent are educable, i.e., capable of learning some basic academic skills such as reading, writing, and arithmetic to the second-, third-, and fourth-grade level. "Educable" retardates can perform unskilled and semiskilled work and can usually main- tain themselves in society, although they may need some supervision when under economic or social stress. Eleven per cent of the total number of retarded persons are considered "trainable." Although they cannot acquire academic skills, they can develop self-help skills and can do repetitive type work in sheltered situations. The remain- ing are so severely retarded that they require total nursing care throughout their lives.[7]

A fourth stereotype is that mental retardation affects only a rela- tively small number of persons and that these should be cared for in institutions. Mental retardation, however, is a condition affecting 5.4 million persons in the United States. Each year 126,000 babies are born who will be recognized as mentally retarded at some time in their lives. Of these, 12,600 will never reach the seven-year intel- lectual level, and 4,200 will spend their lives completely helpless, unable even to care for their own personal needs. Furthermore, some fifteen to twenty million other persons are directly affected by this condition in their families. Only four significant disabling conditions (mental illness, cardiac disease, arthritis, and cancer) exceed mental retardation in prevalence.[8]

At the present time, the care or treatment of the retarded is largely a community problem and not an institutional one. Of these 5,400,-000 persons, approximately 200,000 are cared for in public and private residential facilities. Of the severely retarded, 75 per cent live in the community, while only 25 per cent live in institutions. Of the moderately retarded or "trainable," 85 per cent live in the community, while 99 per cent of the mildly retarded or "educable" reside in the community.[9] Consequently, each denomination has a considerable number of retarded persons within its fellowship. For example, the Missouri Synod of the Lutheran Church estimates that of the approximately 75,000 retarded persons within its communion, 95 per cent reside in the community.

Thus, the church's perspective toward mental retardation includes an acceptance of the current scientific knowledge as to its nature and cause, an appreciation of the uniqueness of retardation as an educational and social problem, recognition of the various levels of retardation, and the awareness that mental retardation is of concern to the local church.

Is the Church Involved?

What is the church in relation to mental retardation? In this new ministry we must first ask what the church must *be* before we ask what it can *do*. More basic than action is the clarification of the church's nature as a ministering community, the underlying attitude toward mentally retarded persons and their families, and the motivation for this ministry.

Nature of the church.—The church's understanding of its own identity as a ministering community determines the nature of its ministry in mental retardation. An emphasis on the church's institutional nature to the exclusion of its missionary function results in two adverse attitudes.

First of all, emphasis is placed on the service which the members render to the church instead of the church's ministry to persons. Such an emphasis ignores the deep needs of parents of retarded children for a ministry of healing, guiding, and sustaining. The inadequacy of this view of the church in relation to mental retardation was demonstrated in one minister's attitude toward a family with a retarded child. The child had been kept at home for several years. His care left little time for his parents to participate in the organizational life of the church. When the child was eventually placed in an institution, the pastor's response was: "I told George [the father] for years that he ought to put that kid in an institution and get back into the church. His family had not been as active as they once were or as they ought to have been." In this situation, the church and pastor should have reached out to support and sustain the family in this emotionally and physically depleting circumstance. Instead, the pastor attempted to make the family feel guilty because of their unavoidable neglect of the church.

Second, the church restricts its ministry to "whole" persons capable of being absorbed into church programs designed for the average. Such an attitude was reflected by the Christian education director who said that he did not want "these persons" (mentally retarded children) in his religious education program. He personally felt that all retarded children should be institutionalized. Furthermore, the pastor of a village church stated that he ministered only to the average and above average in intelligence because these persons were more "responsible" than the below average. By these attitudes, the church isolates itself from persons who are "different." As the Presbyterian report on "The Relation of Christian Faith to Health" says: "Too often it seems that the Church has a low tolerance point for those who are exceptions to the kinds of health and social adjustment which typify the majority of her members."[10]

To effectively minister to the retarded and their families, the church must be a ministering community, responsible for service to all persons, regardless of their ability to respond. The continuing concern of the church is testimony "that God cares and refuses to let go, even when society has exhausted what it knows how to do or the responsibilities it is ready to assume."[11] As a responsible and concerned community, the church is the instrument of healing for the retarded and their families.

Attitude toward retarded persons.—Clarification is further needed in regard to the feelings of church leaders and members toward the retarded. Acceptance of common misconceptions and stereotypes regarding mental retardation has effectively insulated the church from personal involvement, from entering emphatically into the experience of the parents, and from forming personal relationships with retarded persons themselves. The following are examples of the harmful effects of rejecting attitudes.

After addressing a pastor's conference, an institutional chaplain was asked: "How can I help my members have the right attitude toward parents of retarded children? My members even shy away from the parents." The pastor felt that these attitudes undercut the effectiveness of his ministry. In another situation, a minister refused to be physically close to a retarded child in his congregation and was reluctant to visit in the home of the mother. His only ministry was to advise the mother "to put that kid in an institution." Moreover, a church member responded to residents of a state institution attending her church on Sunday night with this comment: "I don't like to be around them. I feel 'creepy' every time I get close to them."

When such attitudes are held, there is no foundation upon which to build a responsible ministry. Two immediate steps are indicated. The first is to clarify the feelings of ministers and church members toward retarded persons. It must be honestly recognized that retarded persons often do generate unpleasant feelings and that the physical deformities of some retardates are repulsive. On a deeper level, contact with the retarded may bring to consciousness unresolved conflict and anxiety. For example, through intensive relationships with the retarded, one must acknowledge his feelings toward limitations and handicaps. This means that one must accept himself as a limited person. Fears about fate and unresolved guilt feelings may also be attached to the retarded. If retardation is associated with moral causes, the whole problem of sin, suffering, and punishment must be faced. In institutions where residents freely talk about being separated from their families, the worker may have to deal with his own unresolved separation anxieties connected with leaving the home of the parents.

Since the ministry of the church is a personal one, nothing less than an admission and clarification of existing attitudes toward retarded persons will do. However, the ministry of the church has a theological foundation. The second step then is to clarify the theological basis for accepting relationships with the retarded. Inherent within the theology and heritage of the church are resources for creating attitudes of understanding, compassion, and acceptance.

Several biblical teachings provide sound guides for developing right attitudes toward retarded persons. First, the belief that man is created in the image of God means that the retarded are persons and not symbols. They are to be understood and accepted as they are rather than what we think or have heard they are. Second, God accepts all men by grace through faith and not by works of righteousness. Since before God all men are limited and in need of healing, any basis for feeling superior to retarded persons is without foundation. Third, God's call is the same for every man. Each person is called into the fellowship of the church through Jesus Christ, to achieve his maximum potential as an individual, and to serve God through his vocation. Fourth, the biblical emphasis on the way of love as the Christian response to human need demands personal involvement as the "rule" for service.

Motivation for ministry.—When previously unacknowledged feelings toward retarded persons are examined in the light of the gospel, then warm and accepting attitudes are free to grow. The process of repentance, however, must also cleanse unworthy motives for ministering to the retarded. As important as recognizing the missionary nature of the church and clarifying rejecting attitudes is the exploration of the church's motivation. Because the church lags far behind other social institutions and agencies, we must examine this sudden concern about the problem of mental retardation. More is required of the church than good intentions. A searching appraisal of motivation is necessary.

Of the motivations prompting the present interest of the churches in mental retardation, at least four defective motives can be discerned. One defective motive is the ministry performed from a sense of duty. The church's sense of "oughtness" is both a weakness and a strength. Sensitivity to human need and self-consciousness as a ministering community has culminated in the church's awareness that the retarded represent a large group of persons almost completely ignored. Such recognition often results in a sense of guilt. Consequently, religious ministries are sometimes provided for the retarded without adequate preparation. For example, a church began a religious education class for the retarded children attending the public school. These children were from a lower socioeconomic group than were the majority of the church members. Their parents did not attend the sponsoring church. After an initial burst of enthusiasm, the church lost interest and was unable to recruit teachers.

A second defective motive is the sponsoring of special religious education classes as an evangelistic method for winning parents who are not Christians, attend another church of the same denomination, or belong to other denominations. Such a ministry, as a concrete expression of love, may result in evangelistic opportunities. This ministry, however, is an end within itself and should not be used as the means to another end; namely, the evangelization of the parents. Those who give careful attention to the religious needs of the parents, however, may see visible results for their labor.

A third defective motive is the sponsoring of religious education classes because parents of retarded persons pressure the church to do so. In its most extreme form, the church simply provides the space and equipment, while the parents serve as teachers, enlist the students, and direct the program. Parents often must call to the church's attention that their child is entitled to religious training which is not being provided, but the church makes the same provisions for the retarded as it does for other members of the church school. In addition to providing space and equipment, the church enlists and elects the teachers and supervises the operation of the special class.

A fourth defective motive is the sponsoring of special classes in order to compete with a neighboring church. This and other defective motives are apparent in the following illustration. The parents of retarded children in an urban church strongly insisted that the pastor and Christian education director establish a special class similar to a neighboring church whose program had attracted considerable attention. The Christian education director insisted that the church proceed cautiously and make careful plans. Tentative plans were formulated, but no census was taken to determine the potential enrolment for such a class. While the education director was out of town, and without his consent, the pastor began the special class. On the next Sunday, more retarded children came than the teaching staff could handle, and additional teachers were hurriedly secured from other classes. However, the responsibility for stabilizing and maintaining this program belonged to the Christian education director, not to the pastor who started it. Impulsive action, preceded by incomplete planning and motivated by pressure from parents and competitiveness with a neighboring church, resulted in a questionable beginning for a ministry which demands a clean heart and a right spirit.

Each of these defective motives stands condemned in the light of Protestant theology. Service which issues from a sense of duty, stereotyped evangelistic concern, parental pressure, or competitiveness is unworthy of the church. Our response of compassion to retarded persons and their families is rooted and grounded in God's movement toward us in Jesus Christ. Our good works show a joyous response to God's salvation. The calling of the Christian man makes him a priest to his brother—a responsibility which he cannot shirk without forsaking his calling. As a member of the body of Christ, the Christian shares the burdens of his brothers and responds to their total needs.

With mental retardation, as with every other social problem, the church's opportunity to minister is a privilege earned and not a right automatically bestowed. The church's struggle to form an identity in relation to these families is a difficult but necessary prerequisite to the rendering of effective and sensitive service. The understanding of the church's nature, the attitude toward the retarded, and the motivation for ministering all determine the extent to which the church can be involved in mental retardation.

What the Church Can Do

At least three features characterize the nature and scope of the church's ministry in mental retardation. First, it is not different from its ministry in other crisis situations or even in good health. Failure to clearly appreciate this basic principle often results in the mistaken assumption that a corps of trained workers is a prerequisite to any involvement by the church. Although ministers routinely offer pastoral services to the physically ill, to couples experiencing marital trouble, and to persons with other personal difficulties, some ministers absolve themselves of responsibility to families affected by mental retardation. They claim they are not "specially trained" for this type of ministry. For example, a minister with graduate training in psychology qualified his answer regarding the church's responsibility in mental retardation by saying, "The minister should take care not to exceed his capacities in such matters." Responsibility was denied in another pastor's claim that much of the church's ministry would have to be beyond the local church level.

Other ministers, however, are more realistic and perceptive regarding the nature of the church's ministry. They rightly understand that the church, by its very nature, is interested in the total life of man, even though it does not have the full answer. As one pastor put it: "The church has responsibility in every area of human need and suffering." Said another, "Mental retardation is an opportunity for the church to minister." Furthermore, in the survey on "The Ministry and Mental Retardation" some clergymen reported having rendered to the retarded and their children the traditional ministries of the church. They offered meaningful pastoral relationships to the parents and made referrals to other professional persons. Services to the retarded included pastoral care, ministry at the time of religious decision, and religious education. Many of the ministers identified some basic theological issues in mental retardation and reported some of the religious dynamics present in the parental response to the birth of a retarded child. Consequently, the church's ministry in mental retardation is essentially the same as in all other realms of life.

Second, the church's ministry must be relevant to the specific problems created by mental retardation. Failure to secure basic information regarding mental retardation may result in an ineffective and ill-advised ministry.

One example is the way in which Christian theology is often related to mental retardation. The doctrine of the sovereignty of God has often been interpreted to mean that God is the cause of mental retardation. A careful reading of the literature on the biological causes of retardation, however, would dispel this primitive belief. One pastor said: "Some of the children are retarded because of the kind of life the parents have lived." In another instance, a minister contended: "The Bible teaches that all sickness, disease, or pain is the result of sin—not always personal sin."

A second example of misunderstanding is evident in the ministry of pastors to the parents of retarded children. Clergymen who have ministered to such parents often indicate a feeling of helplessness. "I felt helpless in one way," confessed a pastor, "that I did not know just the counsel to give or maybe the right suggestions to offer that would be best in each case." Another pastor handled his helplessness by suggesting to the parents that "they get help from people equipped to help." Obviously, these ministers had failed to clarify the areas in which they were competent to function or to identify the needs of parents with which a minister could be of help. Consequently, there is an urgent need for an examination of mental retardation from the perspective of the church's unique ministry.

Third, the ministry of the church in mental retardation must be perceived in a broad and comprehensive fashion. Unfortunately, it is often assumed that the extent of the church's responsibility is to provide special religious education classes for retarded persons. However, the 220 clergymen surveyed overwhelmingly believed that the church has a broad responsibility in mental retardation. A full ministry includes the pastoral counseling of the retarded and their families, a supportive ministry to encourage and strengthen the parents, referrals to community agencies, as well as religious education for the retarded. Furthermore, these ministers indicated that they were already performing several of these ministries and that the religious training of retardates was only one function of the church. The specifically religious role of the church is not restricted to any one facet of its total outreach. Rather, the church's entire ministries and resources are required.

Relating the church's faith and ministry to the special needs of families affected by mental retardation is the first task. What are these needs? How can the church meet them? Exploration of the ministry to the family is the purpose of Part One.

Notes

1. Harold W. Stubblefield, "The Ministry and Mental Retardation," *Journal of Religion and Health*, January, 1964, pp. 136-47.

2. The first contemporary research article treating any aspect of the church's role in mental retardation was published on this date by Howard Schomer, "Religious Ministry to the Mentally Deficient," *American Journal of Mental Deficiency*, July, 1946, pp. 67 f.

3. Rick Heber, "Modifications in the Manual on Terminology and Classification in Mental Retardation," *American Journal of Mental Deficiency*, January, 1961, p. 499. For other material in this discussion I am indebted to Heber's "A Manual on Terminology and Classification in Mental Retardation," Monograph Supplement, *American Journal of Mental Deficiency*, September, 1959, pp. 3-4, and "Mental Retardation: Concept and Classification," *Readings on the Exceptional Child: Research and Theory*, eds. E. Philip Trapp and Philip Himelstein (New York: Appleton-Century-Crofts, 1962).

4. Richard L. Masland, Seymour B. Sarason, and Thomas Gladwin, *Mental Subnormality: Biological, Psychological, and Cultural Factors* (New York: Basic Books, 1958), p. 4.

5. *Ibid.*

6. Heber, *Readings on the Exceptional Child: Research and Theory, op. cit.*, p. 71.

7. Glenn E. Milligan, "Statewide Planning for the Mentally Retarded," *Mind over Matter*, December, 1962, pp. 32-33.

8. "Report of the President's Panel," *American Association of Mental Deficiency Education Reporter*, December, 1962, p. 12.

9. Milligan, *op. cit.*

10. *The Relation of Christian Faith to Health* (Philadelphia: The United Presbyterian Church in the United States of America, 1960), p. 38.

11. Charles D. Kean, *Christian Faith and Pastoral Care* (Greenwich, Conn.: The Seabury Press, 1961), p. 91.

2

Mental Retardation
as a Family Problem

The church's concern with the family dimensions of mental retardation is deeply rooted in historical tradition. Historically, the Christian faith has maintained definite views regarding marriage, the family, and children. The church ministers to persons as family members, not as isolated individuals. Consequently, any crisis which threatens the family falls within the province of the church's concern.

Mental retardation is a family problem long before it ever becomes a problem for the community. Pastors and church members are first involved with the family dimensions, and secondly, with the religious training of retarded children. Thus, a clear understanding of mental retardation as a family problem is essential to the effective functioning of the church. For the church's purpose, three aspects of the family involvement require careful attention.

The Context of Mental Retardation

The birth of a retarded child must be regarded as a crisis situation. How this crisis is met, however, will be determined by the family's response to other crises. Although the retarded child creates almost insurmountable problems, the family responds with its present values, goals, strengths, and weaknesses. Mental retardation is not an isolated problem, detachable from the "context" of the family in which it occurs. Forces within and without the family influence the response to the retarded child and the effect he has on the family.

One of the factors influencing the response of parents toward a retarded child is the emotional health and maturity of the parents

15

themselves. It must be recognized that the presence of a retarded child in a family creates many difficult problems and that the parents often react in a defensive fashion. But, as Mahoney[1] observed, the defensive reaction is usually only temporary in parents who have previously effected a good adjustment in their relationships. As the threat of mental retardation lessens, the parents react in a more realistic fashion. They are then able to do what is best for the child. Supportive counseling, which permits parents to express their feelings and plans for the child, is usually effective.

The defensive reaction will more likely tend to be pathological if the parents, prior to the birth of the retarded child, have not adjusted satisfactorily. Instead of realistically planning for the welfare of the child, the parents meet their own needs through the child. The child becomes a pawn in marital disagreement or a symbol of the defects of one or both of the parents.

The retarded child, for instance, may become a source of friction between the husband and wife. In meeting the child's needs, the wife may neglect the husband. Unable to realistically cope with the situation, the husband responds by spending much time away from the home. Openly or secretly, the parents often blame each other for producing a defective child. Further, the retarded child may become the "scapegoat" upon whom the parents blame their troubles instead of accepting the fact that they had the same problems before the child came.[2]

The retarded child is often used in the service of the neurotic needs of the parents. Having a retarded child meets the needs of some parents to be wanted and useful. The child's need for constant care gives them a purpose in their own lives. As one mother put it: "Nobody in the world ever really needed me except this one little child. Thank God that he will need me forever."[3] In contrast, for other parents the retarded child becomes a concrete symbol of inferiority and failure. One mother said: "I always thought of myself as a failure until I got pregnant, and then I felt I was just as good as anyone else. But after the child came I realized that I had failed in everything, and I didn't want to live any more."[4]

Thus, the effect of the birth of a retarded child on the family is influenced by the emotional health and maturity of the parents. Similarly, the ministry of the church hinges on the nature of the family's response. With some parents, the pastor may participate in their pilgrimage of realistically facing their own feelings and mobilizing resources. If the family becomes chronically defensive, the pastor must bide his time until the family is receptive to help. A pastor, for instance, was unable to render any ministry to a family because he "felt that honest help in this particular case would not have been well received by the parents."

Another significant factor in the parental response is the religious definition of the family and the resultant attitude toward children. In two recent studies, Catholic parents were found to be more accepting of a retarded child than non-Catholics. Farber[5] interpreted his finding as suggesting "that participation in the Catholic Church and/or Catholic definition of home and family life were supportive." Zuk,[6] on the other hand, attributed the Catholic mothers' greater acceptance of a retarded child to their religious teachings regarding parental guilt. Catholic doctrine is explicit that parents should not feel guilty for bearing a retarded child. Instead, Catholic parents are asked to accept the child as a special gift of God. Protestant and Jewish doctrines, however, are not this explicit.

Since the implications of these studies are significant, the specific findings need further elaboration. Farber studied the "effects of a severely mentally retarded child on family integration." He found "little difference in the marital integration of Catholics with a retarded boy at home and those with a boy in an institution." Among non-Catholics, however, "the marriage of parents with a retarded boy at home were more adversely affected than those with a boy in an institution." In short, non-Catholics seem more affected than Catholics in a crisis situation and more benefited when the retardate is institutionalized.

Zuk explored the religious practices of seventy-two mothers and the attitudes toward their retarded children. The Catholic mothers reported themselves and their husbands as more intensive in formalized religious observances than either the Protestant or Jewish mothers. Part two of the questionnaire pertained to the mothers' attitude toward overprotection, discipline, cause of mental retardation, acceptance of diagnosis, and mother's self-fulfilment. On three items Catholic mothers more frequently gave the prejudged response, reflecting greater acceptance of the child. Protestant mothers, more frequently than Catholic mothers, stated that their mission in life was to care for their retarded child. They more often became impatient with their retarded children, and they felt that medical care could make their child normal.

More basic than the attitudes toward retarded children, however, is the attitude of parents toward children in general, child rearing, and homemaking. As a result of the explicit teachings of the Catholic Church concerning children and the family, Catholic parents seem to have retained more traditional views toward the family. They stress the necessity of durable family relationships and regard the bearing of children as a God-ordained responsibility. In contrast, Protestants emphasize the morality of planned parenthood. Although the morality of planned parenthood is not questioned, one wonders what effect this emphasis has on parents who produce a defective child unable to contribute constructively to society. Catholic families also seem to have different values toward child rearing and home-making. Lenski's study[7] of 656 Detroit families revealed that Prot-estant mothers more often than the Catholic mothers felt that chil-dren were burdensome to a greater or lesser degree. In contrast to 68 per cent of these Catholic mothers, who regarded the experience of rearing the child as either "pleasant" or "very pleasant," only 51 per cent of the Protestant mothers fell in these categories. Thus many Protestant mothers tended to find little satisfaction in their role as mothers.

Religious teachings, therefore, may be a significant factor in the parental response to a retarded child. Especially is this true when the religious group values durable family relationships and regards children as persons important in themselves and not as a means for the fulfilment of the parents' ego needs.

Akin to the religious factor in the parental response is the effect of cultural values as represented by social class distinctions. Parents in the lower socioeconomic classes tend to respond differently than those in the higher classes.

Farber's study[8] of approximately five hundred families with a se-verely retarded child isolated two types of responses correlated with social class. The problem confronting parents in the lower socio-economic group revolved around "role-organization"—coping with the additional burden of caring for a retarded child. Since these parents do not usually have high intellectual ambitions for their children, the retardation is often less frustrating to personal ambition and less emotionally disturbing.

A different type of crisis was apparent in the response of parents in the high socioeconomic status. Farber labeled this response the "tragic crisis." These families placed much emphasis on attainment of long-range goals, for which high intellectual functioning is essential. Thus, their problem revolved around the frustration of the aims, aspirations, and anticipated "happy" family life. The retarded child prevents the parents from fulfilling their hopes and goals. Consequently, when high intellectual functioning is incorporated as one of the family's values, genuine acceptance of a child who does not measure up intellectually is quite difficult.

The "tragic crisis" response reflects a standard of values in which children are only genuinely accepted when they contribute to the personal goals of the parents. Ruth Benedict, a cultural anthropologist, contends that American children are not individuals whose rights and tastes are casually respected from birth. Rather, they are "special responsibilities, like our possessions, to which we succumb or in which we glory, as the case may be. They are fundamentally extensions of our own egos and give a special opportunity for the display of authority."[9]

According to Lenski's study, Protestants more often than Catholics hold these values regarding children. For example, Protestants more often than Catholics valued intellectual autonomy in children above obedience. Protestant children were expected to assume responsibility for themselves at an earlier age than Catholic children. Thus Protestants tended to emphasize the qualities in children which facilitates success in the world of work. Consequently, an indication of a family's attitude toward children and its response to a retarded child may be found in its cultural values and religious beliefs. These studies, however, do not warrant widespread generalizations. They point up though the need for further research regarding the relation of religious faith and social class to the response toward a retarded child.

Recognition of the family context of mental retardation inseparably links this problem to the family ministry of the church. In this regard, the church's role becomes preparatory, interpretive, and prophetic. The preparatory phase involves sensitive pastoral care of couples prior to and following the marriage ceremony. As the pastor helps the couple clarify their own emotional needs, their expectations of each other, and form open channels of communication, he strengthens the family's ability to handle crisis situations, including the crisis of mental retardation. An interpretative ministry involves clarifying the Protestant understanding of the nature of marriage and the purpose of the sexual relationship. Current "companionship" views of marriage obscure the biblical understanding of marriage as a covenant under God and as a lifetime commitment to each other. Contemporary casualness toward sexual relationships obscures the biblical teachings that one purpose of the union is the bearing of children. Careful interpretation is also needed concerning the place of children in marriage and the vocational calling of women to be wives and mothers. In marriages where children are unwanted and the mother is discontented in her role as a mother, the crisis of mental retardation is intensified. In its prophetic role, the church challenges harmful attitudes toward children and the use of children to meet the needs of parents. The church should champion the right of children to be valued for what they are in themselves and not what they represent to their parents. Recognition of the personal frustration and the difficult problems which a retarded child brings to a family does not permit us to ignore the idolatrous use to which these children are often put. Children are not born in order that the parents may relive their lives through their accomplishments. Neither are they to be loved only if they enhance the social status of the family. Children—normal and retarded—have the right to be accepted and loved as they are.

The Crisis of Mental Retardation

The nature and extent of the crisis resulting from the birth of a retarded child depends upon the family context in which it occurs. However, a mentally retarded child creates several problems for almost every family. Regardless of the appearances of the family, the pastor and church should be sensitive to common problem areas. Three of the common problems are the process of acceptance, the continuing care of the child, and the effect on the family.

Process of acceptance.—Parental response to a retarded child is best compared to a bereavement reaction. In most instances, a definite pattern can be discerned. The process through which a grief-stricken person moves, as Wayne Oates says, has six discernible steps. He describes these as the shocking blow of the loss in itself; the numbing effect of the shock; the struggle between fantasy and reality; the breakthrough of a flood of grief; selective memory and stabbing pain; and the acceptance of loss and the reaffirmation of life itself.[10]

In at least three ways, however, the response to a retarded child differs from the grief reaction to the death of a family member or loved one. First of all, the parents are not always presented with an accomplished fact as in the death of a family member. Unless the child's retardation is obvious at birth because of physical stigmata, the parents only gradually become aware of the condition. Rosen observed several steps in the development of the mother's understanding of her mentally retarded child. Some of these steps occurred simultaneously or were closely related. The phase of awareness came first.

The mother first experiences that her child is different. In a sample of thirty-six mothers, the child's mean chronological age at which the mothers first made this observation was two years and eight months. Some mothers recognized their child's retarded condition as early as birth or as late as seven years. Next came the phase of recognition in which the mothers were able to acknowledge that the child was retarded. Recognition was followed by the phase of seeking for the cause. After searching to find the reason for the retardation, the mothers then sought to find a cure or relief for the child's retardation. At this point they sought professional services.[11]

The bereavement reaction is different also in that there is no corpse to mourn. The parents grieve over a great loss—their desire for a normal child. Third, the bereavement for many parents is never "worked through." Bearing a retarded child is an event which they never get over. For example, Thurston's study of the emotional reactions of parents of institutionalized cerebral palsied retarded patients found "considerable emotional upset remaining after an average of about ten years had elapsed."[12] Simon Olshansky[13] describes this response as "chronic sorrow." Parents, therefore, should not be expected to shut up their feelings when they once learn that they have a retarded child. They continue to feel sorrow, regardless of the degree of acceptance they evince, and they continue to need opportunities to express their feelings.

Since parents continue to harbor feelings even after acknowledgment of the retarded condition, what is meant by "acceptance" of a retarded child. Acceptance does not mean that parents repress their feelings or that these feelings ever completely disappear. What is hoped for is that parents will acknowledge their feelings, both toward the child and themselves, and realistically plan for the child's future on the basis of the needs of the child, the needs of the family, and the family's resources. Further, the child is assigned a place within the family according to his special needs without becoming the hub around which the entire family revolves. The needs of the other family members are not sacrificed for the retarded child. In short, the child is accepted as he is.

Such acceptance occurs only when parents are free to express their deeper feelings. Our culture and religious groups, however, place moral value upon certain emotions and set limits for their expression. As a result, some feelings such as anger and resentment are repressed altogether.

When parents are free to express their feelings, a fairly predictable pattern of response emerges. Winburn Davis [14] charted this pattern in the parents of retarded children whom he as a social worker interviewed. He observed that all the parents went through the stages of grief, guilt, and resentment before reaching the stage of acceptance. Many parents said that they stopped crying after the birth of their retarded child. After honestly acknowledging their emotions in the presence of an accepting person, however, they were able to cry again. The parents expressed feelings of guilt by asking what they did to have a retarded child. Other emotions expressed were disappointment, fear of the future, failure, shame, repulsion of the child, and hopelessness. The parents able to express these feelings, some after a few interviews and others after three to six months, were freed to move toward a realistic solution of their problem and to accept limited goals for their children.

Some parents never reach this degree of acceptance. In some instances, parents are never able or willing to face the reality of the retarded condition. They completely deny that there is any problem at all. Another type of reaction, in addition to mature acknowledgment or complete denial, is the acknowledgment of the handicap but unrealistic methods of handling it. For example, it may be assumed that changing the circumstances would restore the child to normalcy. The child's failure in school is attributed to his laziness or to an incompetent teacher. The parents overprotect the child—keeping him a baby and thus avoiding the threat that increasing maturity would bring. Unrealistic goals beyond the child's capabilities are set, or the parents adopt a "martyr" attitude, centering everything on the child. Finally, the child may be outright rejected.[15]

The problem of continuing care.—Closely associated with the crisis of acceptance is the crisis created by the child's need for continuing care. In contrast to the eventual independent functioning which normal children attain, the parents can never anticipate the retarded child's being independent and functioning in the community without minimum supervision from some source. Even if he is institutionalized, they will still maintain some contact. As long as the parents live, they will be responsible in some way for this child.

The management of the child varies according to the mental and developmental level. If the child is severely retarded, the family faces a lifetime nursing task. Because the child will never care for his own needs, the family must cope with a prolonged infancy period. If moderately retarded, the child can develop self-help skills and benefit from training in repetitive type work. If a sheltered workshop is available, he may even contribute to his own support, but he will always need supervision and guidance, even in adulthood. A higher level of functioning is expected from the mildly retarded who benefits from academic education and can learn semiskilled and unskilled types of work. Hopefully, as an adult he can function independently with only minimum supervision.

As the moderately and mildly retarded become adolescents and adults, adjustments in management procedures are necessary. At adolescence, the retarded, like normal children, become more autonomous and demand more independence. They often develop sexual interests and manifest aggressive behavior. The family must determine the amount of independence he is ready to assume. For example, is he allowed to go out by himself to the store or around the corner to visit a friend? Like normal adolescents, the retarded person needs companionship, recreational opportunities, and the opportunity for a full life within the boundaries of his limitations. Even mothers who successfully handled the child on a younger level may be threatened by the demands of adolescence. A new assessment of the child's ability is necessitated at each developmental stage.

When adulthood is reached, the retardate will have received the maximum benefit from educational and vocational training. His ability to maintain himself through meaningful work and to develop a wholesome social life will be tested. Parents may be overwhelmed by what adulthood holds for their retarded child. Since the parents by this time are elderly, some decision is necessary regarding the future of the retarded adult. If he is unable to maintain himself, continuing supervision must be provided, either in an institution or in the community.

In considering these two aspects of the crisis of mental retardation, it is obvious that the birth of a retarded child creates numerous problems for parents and that the nature of these problems varies according to the degree of retardation. The parents, first, must accept the reality of the retardation and "work through" their feelings toward this event. Next, they must learn to cope with a child who will always be an infant or who will require special training. Finally, a lifetime program of care and supervision for the child must be planned.

The effect on the family.—Even the birth of a normal child is a possible source of family crisis. Role changes, schedule adjustments, feelings toward the child, and in-law involvements are all possible problem areas. The effect of a retarded child on a family is not significantly different from that of a normal child, though he may intensify problems already present. Thus, in assessing the retarded child's effect on the home it is important to assess the stability of the home, the nature of communication between the parents, and the method of handling problems before the child was born. The retarded child may simply bring to the surface existing problems that were never openly acknowledged.

A mentally retarded child, however, may have an adverse effect on the family. For example, in the parents' struggle to cope with the child and handle their feelings, unresolved conflict and repressed hostility may break through. Instead of mutually supporting one another, the parents blame each other for the tragedy. An atmosphere of suspicion and mistrust develops. Moreover, the child may precipitate a "role-organization" crisis. The care of the child is so demanding that the family is either unable to cope with it or it invests all of its energy and time in caring for the child. When this occurs, the retarded child often has an adverse effect on the normal brothers and sisters. The atmosphere of the home becomes so tense that normal children become emotionally upset. When the retarded child is hyperactive, aggressive, and destructive, the younger siblings may imitate his behavior.

The crisis of mental retardation presents many opportunities for the pastoral care of the pastor. Meaningful involvement with the family, however, necessitates an awareness of the decisions which the parents are required to make in regard to this child. In coping with the problem, parents render value judgments affecting the life of the normal siblings and the parents, as well as the retarded child. These decisions are relevant to the ethical concerns of the church.

Ethical Aspects of Family Decisions

The family's dilemma in planning for the care of a retarded child is compounded by the mixed feelings of the community and by the contradictory advice received from other family members and professional persons. With little consideration for the family's feelings or needs, interested friends and relatives often render general judgments regarding the best course of action for the family. For example, when an infant is obviously retarded at birth, some physicians recommend that the child be immediately institutionalized. In some cases, the mother is discouraged from ever seeing her child. Other physicians, in order to protect the family, blandly assure parents that their retarded child will "outgrow it." Ministers are also guilty of giving similar advice. On the other hand, it is sometimes believed that the ideal family keeps the child at home, regardless of the effect on the family.

The present confusion illustrates the need for a more personal and realistic approach in guiding families affected by mental retardation. Such an approach includes a general perspective encompassing the total situation, knowledge of the significant factors to be considered in arriving at satisfactory decisions, and sensitivity to the ethics of the parent-helper relationship.

What counsel ministers and lay church workers give to parents of retarded children is shaped by the counselor's view of the total problem and basic values. These values and assumptions need to be made explicit. My own point of view is reflected in the following assumptions of Seymour Sarason:

1. The defective child cannot be studied (or be understood) apart from the family and community in which he lives.
2. The problems, adjustments, and potentialities of the defective child's parents and siblings deserve as much attention and treatment as those of the defective child.
3. Institutionalization should not be recommended unless the results to be achieved by such a move cannot be attained by the continued presence of the child in the home.

4. It is the obligation of the community to provide those facilities which will either make institutionalization in many cases unnecessary or postpone it for as long as the child can benefit from the community program.

5. When the defective child for one reason or another adversely affects the functioning of normal people in his environment, one should not accept the situation but should attempt to ameliorate the situation without removal of the child from that environment. When attempts at such amelioration have proved unsuccessful, the needs and potentialities of the normal people should be given precedence over those of the defective child.

6. A decision about institutionalization should be made by someone who has more than a superficial knowledge of the type and quality of available community resources. Whether the decision is to institutionalize or not, such a decision must be based on an intimate knowledge of the institution's goals, program, and effectiveness.[16]

Decisions affecting the retarded child and family cannot be made apart from consideration of the needs of each person involved. No "rule of thumb" applies to every situation. In the parents' decision either to keep the child at home or institutionalize him, Sarason[17] suggests at least four factors that effect the choice.

The first factor is the family relationship and resources. Consideration should be given to the effect the defective child has on the marital relationship and other siblings, the financial resources of the family, the effectiveness of the home environment for meeting the child's total needs, and the age of the parents. A second factor is the neighborhood attitude and acceptance of the child. In many neighborhoods the retarded child is adversely affected by prejudice and ignorance. On the other hand, the retarded child by his behavior often provokes rejection and ill feeling. The availability of community resources is another factor. Are there professional workers to guide the parents in the management of the child? Are there adequate educational and vocational facilities? Are there recreational facilities? A fourth factor is the adequacy of the institutional program. Each institution, public or private, must be judged on the basis of the program and staff and attitude toward retarded children.

Removal of a retarded child from the home is the exception rather than the rule. It is often necessary though if the child drastically disrupts the family, needs excessive care and supervision, or requires specialized training. Under no circumstances should the family be advised either to keep the child at home or to remove him simply because "it is the thing to do." These kinds of decisions are to be made only after a careful investigation of all the pertinent facts.

Families, however, do not often arrive at these decisions apart from consultation with professional persons, such as physicians, psychiatrists, psychologists, social workers, schoolteachers, nurses, clergymen, and others. In acknowledging the importance of professional services, a mother stated: "The greatest single need of parents of mentally retarded children is constructive professional counseling at various stages in the child's life which will enable the parents to find the answers to their own individual problems to a reasonably satisfactory degree."[18]

Since the need for parent counseling has only recently been recognized, many parents have received inept, inaccurate, and harmful advice from professional workers of almost every discipline. Consequently, ministers, religious education directors, and Sunday school teachers who work with parents of retarded children need an ethical perspective to govern the parent-helper relationship.

The helping relationship begins with sensitivity to the parents' feeling, emotional involvement, and sense of responsibility to the child. Appreciation of "hidden" emotions, such as guilt, hostility, shame, and embarrassment, which many parents harbor, permits the religious worker to be patient even when he does not understand the parents' response. Only an honest, straightforward relationship elicits trust from parents. It is not wise to hide information nor to be dishonest regarding the child.

Only the parents have the right to make final decisions affecting them and their child. Since the parents are ultimately responsible, the only valid decisions are those which they make.

No one professional worker usually possesses the final solution to the parents' problems. Many resources are available to assist the parents to secure an adequate diagnosis, to plan for the child's future, and to counsel the parents themselves. Parents of retarded children have the same need as other parents for assurance that they are effective and competent in rearing their child.

The function of the worker with parents of retarded children is not limited to supplying information. His first task is to help the parents help themselves by accepting the reality of the total situation, including the reality of their own feelings and the handicap of their child. In helping the parents clarify all the relevant factors in their circumstances, the counselor frees them to make responsible decisions regarding their child with a minimum of anxiety and guilt.

The crisis which a retarded child creates, such as acceptance, continuing care, effect on the family, and ethical decisions clearly calls for a pastoral ministry. In point of time, the church's ministry is first to the parents and second to the retarded child himself. This emphasis in no way denies the importance of an organized Christian education program for the mentally retarded. What is recognized is that the primary ministry, as to time and to urgency of need, is to the family. Without face-to-face involvement with the parents, the ministry is superficial and often irrelevant. Consequently, mental retardation must be recognized as a crisis which often shakes a family to the very depths. The church cannot be less concerned with this crisis than with other crisis situations to which it traditionally ministers. Mental retardation as a family problem is the first "point of contact" with the church. Failure to recognize this results in a ministry which comes too late and ignores the most pressing needs.

Notes

1. Stanley C. Mahoney, "Observations Concerning Counseling with Parents of Mentally Retarded Children," *American Journal of Mental Deficiency*, July, 1958, pp. 85-86.

2. *Ibid.*, p. 83.

3. Joseph Michaels and Helen Schucman, "Observations on the Psychodynamics of Parents of Retarded Children," *American Journal of Mental Deficiency*, January, 1962, p. 572.

4. *Ibid.*, p. 570.

5. Bernard Farber, "Effects of a Severely Mentally Retarded Child on Family Integration," Monograph, *Society for Research in Child Development* (Antioch Press, 1959).

6. G. H. Zuk, *et al.*, "Maternal Acceptance of Retarded Children: A Questionnaire Study of Attitudes and Religious Background," *Child Development*, September, 1961, pp. 525 f.

7. Gerhard Lenski, *The Religious Factor* (Anchor Books ed.; Garden City, N.Y.: Doubleday & Co., Inc., 1963).

8. Bernard Farber, "Effects of a Severely Mentally Retarded Child on the Family," *Readings on the Exceptional Child: Research and Theory*, eds. E. Philip Trapp and Philip Himelstein (New York: Appleton-Century-Crofts, 1962), chap. 17.

9. Ruth Benedict, *Patterns of Culture* (New York: Mentor Book, 1946), p. 213.

10. Wayne E. Oates, *Anxiety in Christian Experience* (Philadelphia: The Westminster Press, 1955), pp. 52-54.

11. Leonard Rosen, "Selected Aspects in the Development of the Mother's Understanding of Her Mentally Retarded Child," *American Journal of Mental Deficiency,* January, 1955, pp. 522 f.

12. John R. Thurston, "Attitudes and Emotional Reactions of Parents of Institutionalized Cerebral Palsied Retarded Patients," *American Journal of Mental Deficiency,* September, 1960, p. 234.

13. Simon Olshansky, "Chronic Sorrow: A Response to Having a Mentally Retarded Child," *Social Casework,* April, 1962, pp. 190-93.

14. Winburn Davis, "Emotional Acceptance of Mental Retardation," an address to the Southern Baptist Conference on Guidance and Counseling, Nashville, Tennessee, September 25, 1962.

15. Leo Kanner, "Parents' Feelings About Retarded Children," *Counseling and Psychotherapy with the Mentally Retarded,* eds. Chalmers L. Stacey and Manfred F. DeMartino (Glencoe, Ill.: The Free Press, 1957), pp. 388-89. Edward L. French and J. Clifford Scott, *Child in the Shadows: A Manual for Parents of Retarded Children* (New York: J. B. Lippincott Co., 1960). chap. 2.

16. Seymour B. Sarason, *Psychological Problems in Mental Deficiency* (3rd ed.; New York: Harper & Bros., 1959), pp. 354-55.

17. *Ibid.,* pp. 347-54.

18. Mrs. Max A. Murray, "Needs of Parents of Mentally Retarded Children," *American Journal of Mental Deficiency,* May, 1959, p. 1084.

3

The Pastoral Care of Parents
of Retarded Persons

The unique ministry of the church to the parents of mentally retarded persons is grounded in its nature as a caring fellowship and interpreter of crucial life events. This chapter, therefore, focuses on pastoral *care* rather than pastoral counseling, since the term "care" designates the total caring ministry of the church. Counseling denotes a structured one-to-one relationship in which a person acknowledges a need for help and assumes some initiative for securing it. A pastoral care ministry does not await the initiative of the parents nor does it involve just the pastor. Rather, the entire membership is involved in all the ways that the church traditionally cares for persons.

In mental retardation, as in other crises, the church's ministry begins with concern, understanding, and involvement. When persons realize that the pastor will accept their feelings and participate in their struggles, they feel free to share deep concern with him. The following case study demonstrates the concerns which parents of retarded children bring to a warm and accepting pastor.

Thirty minutes before the Sunday evening worship service, the superintendent of the Sunday school came to the pastor's study. Mr. Jones is the father of a retarded infant. Although the Joneses wanted children, they were married five years before the first child was born. They now have four children; the youngest is five months old and obviously retarded. In the early part of the discussion, some of Mr. Jones's personal problems in both the Sunday school and his home came to light. He acknowledged that he had been very demanding of the other church members. Also, he had just quit a second job that kept him away from home at night. Now that he has more time

30

at home, his family is more relaxed, and he is able to help his wife with the four children. His concern about his retarded infant enters the conversation when the pastor inquires about Mrs. Jones and the children.

JONES: I am glad that you asked that. K.'s condition has me worried. In fact, sometimes I feel all confused about it.

PASTOR: In what way?

JONES: You remember when you went to the hospital with me the day after K. was born, the day that we talked with Dr. R. and Dr. S. right after the operation on K.

PASTOR: Yes.

JONES: Well, they said that K. was a mongoloid. I just couldn't believe it, so we have gone to two other doctors and they don't agree.

PASTOR: I can see why you would be confused.

JONES: You have never said what you think—that is, if he is or not.

PASTOR: Just what led you to doubt the opinions of Dr. R. and Dr. S.? You had the best doctors one could have.

JONES: The reasons that they gave just were not convincing.

PASTOR: Have you thought of returning to Dr. S. now that K. is almost six months older?

JONES: Dr. T. did suggest this.

PASTOR: Perhaps this would be your best bet. It might put your mind at ease. Maybe you ought to call Mr. D. since he and his wife are facing the same problem.

JONES: Why do you think God let something like this happen?

PASTOR: You ask a very difficult question. First, let me make a suggestion. Human life at times is revealed in its hardest ways but only a realistic view can help us. If your child is diagnosed as a retarded child you will be helped by recognizing whatever limitations there may be. The last time I was in your home you mentioned K. was unable to lift himself up and had trouble with control of his tongue. Recognize these limitations and set your goals in accord with these limitations. Your Christian faith will help you here. In talking with G., I have found her to be applying her faith very well. But, she needs your support and that is the reason for her not being as moody lately, with your encouragement.

(At this time the minister of music opens the door and informs the pastor that it is time to begin the evening service.)

JONES: I am sorry that I have taken so much of your time.

PASTOR: That is quite all right. I do hope that you will talk with me again about this. There is something strange about suffering. The apostle Paul speaks about joy in suffering—that something gratifying comes from it. I am sorry that I must leave but I am going to bring over a little book for you by Dale Evans, called *Angel Unaware*. She speaks of her child as a special child. *(The pastor closed the interview with a brief prayer.)*

What does this interview reveal about the needs of parents which can be met by the pastoral care ministry of the church? This father presented at least three concerns which are clearly within the province of the church's traditional ministry. These relate to the management of problems created by the retarded condition, the theological dimensions of mental retardation, and the need for fellowship and support. Hence, effective pastoral care must give heed to all three of these concerns.

Management of Problems Created by Mental Retardation

The first pastoral care opportunity arises from the parents' concern over the problems created by the retarded condition. Three factors, however, condition the pastor's role. One is the way in which the pastor first learns about the retarded condition. In one survey the clergymen most often learned of the retardation during a routine pastoral call in the home or were approached by the parents. A smaller percentage became aware of the retardation when the child created problems in some church organization or else heard about it through community sources. The problem here is that of initiative. Does the pastor approach the parents, or does he wait until the family's problems become so great that they seek him out?

A second factor is the stage in the development of the child at which the minister learns of the condition. In chapter 2 it was recognized that the kind of help the family needs varies according to the developmental level of the child. In the survey, pastors learned that a child was retarded through the parents' concern over the child's slow development, recognized the retardation at birth, when the family considered institutionalization of the child, or when the child presented behavior problems.

A third factor is the family's reaction and adjustment to the problem. In some instances the family has already adjusted to the problem or received professional help when the minister first meets the family. In other situations, however, the family's unwillingness "to face up to the problem" prevents the minister's effecting any ministry at all.

What the pastor may mean to the parents is determined by the nature of the problems presented by the retarded child and the family's receptiveness to help. As a general rule, the pastor may be of significant help to parents of mentally retarded persons at three stages.

Recognition and acceptance of the retardation.—Parents first need careful and sensitive pastoral attention in the initial recognition and acceptance of the retardation. Suspicious or fully aware that their child is not normal, parents may seek out the pastor as a source of comfort and counsel, as did Mr. Jones. In this situation the pastor wisely set the problem of the retarded child in a family context. Recognizing that the birth of a child is a pastoral care situation, he visited the hospital with the father the day after the child was born and knew from birth that the child was not normal. His knowledge of the family further alerted him to the father's refusal to accept equal responsibility with the mother for the care of the children. Conflict already existed in the home before the retarded child was born. Consequently, the pastor recognized that some of the problems supposedly created by the retarded child were simply an intensification of existing problems.

With regard to the retarded infant, Mr. Jones seems to be grappling with two problems. First, he is still in the "process" of recognizing that his child is retarded. He has not yet really accepted it. The second problem is the relation of mental retardation to his religious faith, which we will treat in a later section. The pastor, at least in the first part of the interview, allows the father to express his feelings of confusion. Wisely, the pastor refuses to be drawn into the argument regarding the doctors' disagreement on the diagnosis but seeks instead to mobilize Mr. Jones to return to the doctor for another consultation. Recognizing that the family needs emotional support to sustain them through this crisis, the pastor suggests that Mr. Jones contact another family who also has a retarded child. In concluding this unscheduled interview, the pastor makes himself available for future conversations.

Not all families, however, seek out the pastor. The pastor then must assess the parents' need and take initiative toward them. When confronted with this choice, some men, oriented toward nondirective pastoral counseling, are tempted to forsake their traditional pastoral care function. For instance, a divinity school student pastor asked this writer what he could do in regard to the parents of retarded children in his church who had not brought any of their problems to him. I replied that if he continued to see himself as a nondirective therapist there was nothing he could do. But if he could activate his role as a Christian pastor then he could move toward his people. Another minister, who had extensive graduate training in psychology, justified his failure to minister to a family with a retarded child in this fashion. "Being nondirective and knowing the parents knew of my qualifications, I left any attempts at counseling up to their initiation, and they made none."

A pastor cannot allow his people to carry the burden of a retarded child without at least acknowledging an awareness of the situation. In taking the initiative, the pastor does not ignore the right of the parents to make final decisions, nor does he force his services when parents obviously do not want them. The general principle underlying all helping relationships is still operative. However, there are some concrete ministries a pastor can offer.

On learning that a family was disturbed at the birth of a child who showed indications of mental retardation, one pastor visited the family and assured them of his personal concern and availability. When the retardation was confirmed, the pastor took from the church library several books on the love and care of the mentally retarded. The pastor continued to visit in the home, seeking to involve the family in the activities of the church. Further, he related this family to another family with a like situation. The pastor felt that this relationship was good for both families. Later the parents joined the local unit of the council for mentally retarded children.

In other situations, the pastor may choose to work through another couple with a retarded child instead of making a direct approach himself. One pastor who heard that a family was frantic at the confirmation of retardation in their infant asked a family in the congregation with a similar experience to visit. Later when the family wanted to talk, the pastor made himself available. This strategy enables parents to identify with other persons who have made a healthy adjustment in analogous circumstances.

In addition to involvement through either the parents or pastor's initiative, a third way in which a pastor makes contact is through referrals from doctors and other professional persons. From the pastoral perspective, referral usually means referral from the pastor to another helping profession. However, ministers also receive referrals. For instance, a pastor, publicly involved in providing community services for the mentally retarded, received a call from a doctor requesting a visit to a family whose three-year-old had just been confirmed as retarded. The clergyman visited the parents and related them to another family with a retarded child. Since these parents were not members of his church, he worked with their pastor to help him help the family. Later he related both the pastor and the family to the local council for retarded children.

At the stage of recognition and acceptance of the retardation, the pastor performs several distinct functions. He is a person with whom the family is free to talk without fear of reproach. When parents of retarded children seek out the doctor or other professional persons, it usually indicates that they have localized the problem and identified persons who can help them. The minister though is often involved when the family only suspects that something is wrong. With awareness of the family's need and with enough emotional distance to be somewhat objective, the pastor enables the parents to bring the problem into sharp focus. This means that the pastor refers the family to other professional persons, such as physicians and psychologists, for an adequate diagnosis of the child's condition and for continued counsel regarding the management of the child. Parents may resist acknowledging that a problem is serious enough to consult professional persons. But the pastor should not support them in deception or denial regarding the problem. Finally, the pastor relates the family to other families with a retarded child, provided they have made a healthy adjustment.

Sensitive pastoral and professional care at the stage of recognition and acceptance prepares the family to more adequately meet other crises arising from the continued care of the child. Thus the work of the pastor does not cease when the family "accepts" the retarded condition.

Management of the child in the home.—Parents need pastoral attention in the management of the retarded child at home. Pastoral strategy is determined by the seriousness of the problems and the family's response to them.

The following excerpts from a pastoral interview demonstrate that continued care of the child often creates severe emotional and physical strain which affects adversely the relationship of the husband, wife, other siblings, and in-laws. A six-year-old with moderately severe retardation and an approximate IQ of 39 was brought to an evaluation clinic for further studies. The parents, in their late twenties, were high school graduates and active church members.

Their other child, a five-year-old son, was developing normally. After the clergyman identified himself as a Protestant minister, working with the Evaluation Clinic, he began the interview:

MINISTER: Have you folks talked with a minister about your situation?
HUSBAND: Not really. Her father and brother are ministers and we have talked with them, but this was more in a family way.
MINISTER: It wasn't a counseling type of situation?
HUSBAND: No, they are too close and involved for that. You know how grandparents can see no wrong in grandchildren. Well, it is hard for them to recognize that Junior is retarded. They just can't be objective.
MINISTER: I imagine that Junior's development causes you much concern.
HUSBAND: Yes, you don't get upset when a normal child makes a mistake. Johnny [the sibling] makes mistakes now and then and I just accept them, but every time Junior makes a mistake or fails to measure up, it upsets me.

.   .   .   .

MINISTER: This has been most difficult for you, Mrs. Tucker, and even more than you feel able to bear.
WIFE: Yes, I've been in for six years. I would give anything to get away, just for a little while.
HUSBAND: Baby sitters don't understand. These young girls come in and sit down with a book and then Junior goes into a rage. If they would only pay him some attention to start with, he would co-operate and not give a bit of trouble.
MINISTER: Do the grandparents live close enough to help?
HUSBAND: It just doesn't work. If Junior wants ten drinks in five minutes, he gets them. They will not correct him and so it is murder for a couple of days after he has been with them.
WIFE: Thomas [husband] gets out and goes to work. He just doesn't understand how I feel.
HUSBAND: I don't like to do anything without the family. I can't go off and leave the boys. If we do anything I prefer to do it as a group. This is the way I have been raised. We always did things as a family. To go off without them is like leaving your legs at home.
MINISTER: I see here two ideas which are really separating you as husband and wife. Possibly Junior has become the center of the home rather than a member in the home.
WIFE: This is true. It is beginning to affect Johnny. He wants to go out and play with his friends. But to keep Junior from crying, we call him back home to play with him.
MINISTER: Is this fair to Johnny?
WIFE: No, it isn't. But Junior cannot go with him, since he doesn't understand the danger of the street. He couldn't go without Johnny.

HUSBAND: There would be no thought about it if he were a normal child. I had to come back and play with my little sister many times.

MINISTER: The difference is in whether it is a temporary or permanent situation.

WIFE: Yes, Thomas, yours was only temporary, where with Johnny it's different.

MINISTER: Maybe Junior will have to learn through experience that Johnny cannot always play with him. It may be as hard on you as it is on Junior. Sometimes these answers are not easy.

WIFE: Sometimes I feel like there are no answers.

.   .   .   .

MINISTER: To summarize, I hear you express deep feelings of a longing for understanding and help. In a sense your marriage has become divided over Junior. It is difficult for you to communicate with each other—to understand and be understood. This experience can serve to move you apart or it can bring you closer together. As a minister, I want to express my concern and to say that God cares about your marriage and understands the complexities of your problems. We do not know the future so you will have to start where you are now and work one step at a time—together, as a team—knowing that God is with you. Instead of Junior's being the center of the home and your lives revolving around him, you will have to function as a family of which Junior is a member. Other members may function independently at times which is necessary. After six years, I can see how you might be discouraged. Yet I trust that together you will be able to find some satisfactory solutions.

WIFE: I hope so. I can't go on this way.

HUSBAND: Thank you for talking with us.

MINISTER: Is there anything you would like to say? Possibly, if you find a need to continue, your pastor or an understanding friend through a Council for Retarded Children could talk with you.

A close examination of this interview reveals a seriously disturbed family. The retarded child's need for continued care has created several problems with which the family is unable to cope. As a result, there is a lack of understanding and communication between the parents.

One of the most obvious problems is the social isolation of the family. Although the parents are active church members and have had a retarded child for six years, they have formed no meaningful relationship to a minister. Members of the church have not recognized the parents' need for relief from the constant care demanded by the child. The grandparents, unable to accept the retarded condition, are so permissive with the child that the mother's efforts to discipline are undermined. Because of the extreme social isolation, the parents are completely exhausted, particularly the mother.

A second problem is the disagreement between the husband and wife regarding the retarded child's place in the home. As the minister rightly observed, Junior has become the center of the home, with the entire family revolving around him. The minister also noted that the father identified very closely with the retarded son and defends him against the mother who seems to side with the normal child. At one place the father expressed dissatisfaction with the normal sibling because he is able to excel. While the father apparently cares very deeply for Junior, he is far from "accepting" the limitations of a defective son. The father has only "partial awareness" of the retarded condition. The mother seems to have "considerable awareness" and recognizes that the needs of the whole family should not be subordinated to the needs of the retarded child. For instance, the mother acknowledges that it is not right to keep the normal sibling at home in order to play with Junior, while the father feels that this is a reasonable expectation.

A third problem which results from the previous two is the sheer hopelessness and futility which the mother feels. Constantly supervising a six-year-old functioning as a two-year-old has completely depleted the mother's strength. Coupled with the demands of the child is the seeming insensitivity of the father to the mother's need for relief from this burden. Instead of taking his wife out of the house, away from the stress and strain of caring for a retarded child, he insists that Junior accompany them everywhere they go. What really makes the mother feel hopeless, however, is the knowledge that there may never be any relief, because this child will require close supervision as long as he lives.

When the pastor confronts a family having difficulty managing a retarded child, he should be guided by several "rules of thumb." Every family situation, of course, is different. Appreciation of the family's emotional involvement is the first rule. The parents in the previous interview had reached an impasse, both in their relationship with each other and in the management of the retarded child. They no longer communicated with nor understood each other's needs. More than an intellectual or advice-giving approach is required if the pastor is to effectively minister to couples facing this problem.

The pastor's second "rule of thumb," therefore, is to help the parents clarify their feelings and to localize specific problem areas for which relief can be secured. In the previous case, the minister's strategy was to allow the parents to verbalize their feelings. Both the mother and father expressed feelings of frustration in regard to the child and conflicts between themselves. Since this would be his only contact with the couple, the minister interpreted in a straightforward fashion his impressions of the problem areas. His summary seemed to reflect the mother's feelings, but the father only politely acknowledged the comments. Whether the minister should have been this direct is a moot question. Nevertheless, his willingness to be involved with and committed to the interests of this couple may have enabled them to communicate more freely between themselves.

The minister, however, terminated the interview prematurely. After helping the parents clarify some of the problems which they were facing, he then only briefly mentioned other resources available in their home community. Thus, a third pastoral "rule of thumb" is to help the family locate and mobilize resources. Since this will be a problem of long duration, the parents need to locate dependable persons to whom they can turn in times of crisis or for support in carrying out routine tasks. One such person should be their own pastor. In this situation, it appears that they will have to take the initiative in informing the pastor of their need. On the other hand, the pastor may just be waiting for them to express a desire for help.

Another resource person is the family doctor who not only cares for the physical needs of the child but is concerned for the entire family. In the local council for retarded children are sympathetic parents with similar experiences. These persons can be a community of healing for parents willing to acknowledge their difficulties. Also, this organization can guide parents to day care centers, special education classes, homemaker services, and baby sitters.

The pastor must be sensitive to the complexities of the total situation and committed to the interests of all the family members. While the pastor often "knows" more than he communicates to the family, he is not a passive bystander. His commitment to a particular family means participation in their anxieties and frustrations and respect for the family's sense of responsibility for the care of the child.

Placement of the child outside the home.—Some retarded children, however, cannot be managed at home. The third stage at which

5

parents need pastoral attention is in the decision to remove the child from the home. Attempts of some parents to institutionalize a retarded child is an obvious evasion of responsibility. In many families, though, the removal of the child from the home is clearly necessary for the protection of the child and the emotional health of the parents and siblings.

Pastors must avoid the pitfall of offering advice on the basis of their feelings without careful consideration of the parents' feelings. When this happens, the minister eliminates himself as a source of help. For instance, a guest minister concluding a worship service in a community church noticed a lady who remained seated with her child after everyone else began leaving. Observing that the child was severely handicapped, he introduced himself to the mother and expressed an interest in her son and his condition. She responded immediately that he was severely retarded. His condition was further complicated by a lack of motor control and a heart defect. The visiting minister then reached for the child and took him in his arms as he would a normal child. The surprised mother commented that most people seemed afraid of him.

During the following week while visiting with the pastor of the church, the guest minister inquired about the lady with the retarded child. "Yes," the pastor replied, "now there is a pathetic case. She had another child who died in an institution. Also, her husband died recently. We've tried to get her to put the boy away, but she won't do it. She says he is her responsibility. I'll tell you, my heart goes out to her. When we first moved here, I just couldn't stand to look at the child. He slobbers and makes those weird sounds. I really don't see how she stands it."

Naturally the pastor's complete rejection and misunderstanding of the mother's feelings were unconsciously communicated to her. Later the mother openly expressed to the guest minister her dismay at the pastor's attitude. Since that time she has turned to the other minister instead of her own pastor for counsel in deciding how to plan for her son's future.

The removal of a retarded child from a home is not as easily accomplished as the pastor believed. While the pastor was completely repulsed by the child, the mother loved him very deeply and felt a mother's responsibility to care for him. Since her husband and other child were dead, the retarded child was all she had left. All of these qualifying conditions were missed by the pastor.

Counseling parents who are considering placing a retarded child or adult in a residential facility involves the pastor in several functions. One function is simply to listen to the parents and to clarify their motivations and reasons for wanting to remove the child from the home. In this way the pastor helps the parents make a valid decision which they can live with through the years. The widowed mother of several children approached a pastor regarding the advisability of placing her retarded child in an institution. She wanted to marry again, but her fiance refused to assume responsibility for a severely retarded child, although he was quite willing to be a father to the normal children. During the interview, the mother did not arrive at a decision, nor did the pastor suggest one to her. She later reported that the child's grandparents agreed to assume responsibility for his care.

The pastor is often able to place the family in contact with the proper community or state agencies. A pastor who had just moved to a new church visited a family in the church membership. One of the children was retarded and a severe management problem. Although the family had considered placing the child in an institution, they were unaware of available facilities. The pastor called the chaplain of a state hospital who arranged for him to talk with a social worker and to make an appointment for the family. In this particular instance, the pastor located resources already available to the family but which they did not know about.

In other instances, the minister may need to suggest institutionalization. This is one alternative which the family should consider when it becomes obvious that the retarded persons can no longer live at home. The pastor does not make the decision for the parents, but he presents it as a possible option.

When the parents responsibly decide to place a retarded person in a residential facility, the pastor should support this decision. Assurance that the parents have made a proper decision in light of all the known facts alleviates many guilt feelings that they may have over forsaking their own flesh and blood. Thus, a pastor who had previously discussed the matter with the family, visibly demonstrated his support by accompanying the parents and the child to the institution for the admission. His presence at this distressing time was quite meaningful to the parents.

Removal of a retarded child from his home creates, for the parents, a bereavement situation, accompanied by mixed emotional responses. The family is often relieved to be free from the constant care and supervision required by a retarded person. They may, however, have extreme guilt feelings regarding the placement and a sense of inadequacy as parents because they were unable to keep the child at home. The pastoral role of clarification and support continues after the placement in order to help the family live with the decision which they have made.

Pastoral care of parents at this stage involves the minister in several tasks. These vary according to the mental and chronological development of the retardate and the family's response to this event. Pastoral attention is needed at the initial recognition and acceptance of the retardation, in the management of the retarded child at home, and when it is necessary to remove the child from the home. Pastoral strategy includes listening to and clarification of the parents' feelings, referral to community and professional resources, and relating the family to persons with a similar experience. Ministering to the family at this stage enables the pastor to deal with the theological problems associated with the birth of a retarded child.

Theological Dimensions of Mental Retardation

As Mrs. Max A. Murray recognized, one need of parents is the resolution of the theological conflicts which arise in their minds at the birth of a retarded child. That a child will remain a mental cripple for the rest of his life may place parents, at least in their own feelings, outside the providence of God's mercy and justice, shatter their belief in God, or overwhelm them with a sense of guilt.[1] With few exceptions, pastoral care literature has scarcely recognized that this problem exists. Indeed, professional workers in mental retardation tend to be more aware of these theological problems than do ministers. The literature on parent counseling by psychiatrists, psychologists, and social workers is replete with illustrations of parental guilt, estrangement, and searching for the ultimate meaning of this event.

Helping parents deal with their theological concerns requires recognition of mental retardation as a theological problem as well as a medical, psychological, educational, and social one. Any event which provokes profound anxiety, personal guilt, and raises questions regarding the moral nature of the universe is a religious problem. Moreover, Christian theology is dynamically related to mental retardation. Religious beliefs influence the parents' response to the birth and care of a retarded child and may have either helping or hindering power. Religion thus may serve as a constructive and strengthening force. It may also be used to impede acceptance and realistic handling of the problem. Consequently, an effective and helpful ministry requires the willingness to creatively relate Christian theology to the human situation rather than pronouncing "eternal truths" without recognition of the context to which they are addressed.

Careful pastoral attention is needed in regard to the theological interpretation of the cause of mental retardation, the parents' sense of personal responsibility and guilt, and the effect of the birth of a retarded child on the religious faith of the parents.

Interpretations of the cause of mental retardation.—The almost inevitable reaction of parents to the confirmation of mental retardation in an infant or child is: "Why did this happen?" This often yields to other responses. "What did I do to cause this to happen?" "Why did God cause this to happen?" Faced with such questions, the minister is tempted to give an answer. However, theological explanations of mental retardation tend either to obscure and misinterpret some aspect of Christian theology or ignore the current biological understanding of the causes of retardation. Mental retardation, like all other manifestations of natural evil, must be regarded as both under God's sovereignty and as a mystery which cannot be explained. Limitations, pain, and suffering are woven into the fabric of human existence and cannot be understood as coming directly from the hand of God. We must work after the fact of human suffering as to its ultimate meaning. "Christian faith in providence," says Bishop Aulén, "does not attempt to give a theoretical explanation of evil." [2] The pastor, therefore, must be ready to sympathetically but firmly challenge parents' erroneous theological explanations.

One such theological explanation is the belief that mental retardation is the punishment of God. As Wayne E. Oates says, one reaction to inevitable suffering, such as birth injuries or congenital deformities, "is the persistent primitive need to think of God as an enemy who inevitably visits the sins of the fathers on the sons, whether he does or not!" [3]

For instance, Mr. Tucker attributed his son's retardation to his own lack of Christian commitment.

HUSBAND: I don't know, but sometimes I feel that if we had been the kind of persons that God wants us to be, it wouldn't have happened.

MINISTER: In what way do you find this so?

HUSBAND: Oh, we are Christians and go to church, but we have backslid and aren't as close as we ought to be. I believe that if we would become the kind of persons that God wants us to be that he would cure Junior.

MINISTER: Do you feel that you can live up to that expectation?

HUSBAND: Yes, I do.

WIFE: I don't feel that way about it. There are lots of people who have retarded children and we are as good as most people. I don't see that we have done anything to merit this. I can't understand why it had to happen to us of all people. Some people are better able to take these things than others.

Mr. Tucker thought of God as a stern judge who expects perfection from his people, rewarding the obedient with good and punishing the offenders with evil. Even now he believes that if he measured up to God's expectations and had enough faith, God would heal his son. In a real sense, he accepts the retardation as their just punishment for not being "the kind of persons that God wants us to be." His wife, as did the minister, rightly challenges this primitive view that suffering always results from sin.

A second theological explanation also attributes mental retardation to an act of God, but with a different emphasis. The Christian doctrine of the sovereignty of God is interpreted to mean that God is the direct cause of every event in life. The underlying assumption of this view makes God the cause of suffering and explains every unfortunate event as a "disguised blessing," which eventually redounds to the glory of God and the good of man.

Dale Evans Rogers' *Angel Unaware* is the most popular representation of this viewpoint. In writing of her "mongoloid" daughter who died at two years of age, Mrs. Rogers says: "I believe with all my heart that God sent her on a two-year mission to our household, to strengthen us spiritually and to draw us together in the knowledge and love and fellowship of God."[4] Similarly, in *The Exceptional Child and the Christian Community*, Hilmar Sieving says that every child is born to serve a specific purpose. This is the "eternal point of view" from which to approach mental retardation. He believes that his own severely retarded son was sent for an eternal purpose which may be "to temper us, to give us patience, to help us speak up to others on behalf of our own and similar problems, to make and keep us humble, to teach us a greater measure of love and faith in the eternal Lord God." [5]

Such an explanation must be challenged on both theological and empirical grounds. The Christian understanding of God is that he is the friend of the injured and handicapped rather than the cause of their suffering. God does not work his will for one person through the deforming of another. Moreover, the suffering of mental retardation, as will be demonstrated in the following section, may be destructive as well as redemptive. Whereas Mrs. Rogers and Mr. Sieving handled their problems redemptively, the suffering of mental retardation has been destructive of the physical, emotional, and spiritual health of countless parents and siblings. The experience of a few parents should not be taken as normative for all parents.

Finally, the ultimate religious solution to mental retardation, according to Dorothy Garst Murray, a mother of a retarded child, is not found in answer to "Why did this thing happen to me?" but rather in answer to "How can I best use what happened to the glory of God and my neighbor's good?" Thus, the task of the pastor is not to give neat theological answers to parents' questions of why. Rather, he is a fellow pilgrim with the family as together they discover, "What is the will of God for my family and this child in the light of our present circumstances?"

A third theological explanation to be challenged regards mental retardation as the result of a hereditary taint or a defective stock. Although now discredited, this view was widely accepted around the turn of the century and has some affinity to one interpretation of "original sin." In this approach, mental retardation is indirectly attributed to the fall of Adam; all suffering and pain entered the human race through original sin. Adam's state before the fall, it is argued, included physical excellence as well as moral innocence. His fall involved the human race in imperfections, disease, and suffering. As a consequence, all evil and suffering result from either personal or corporate sin. The end result of this explanation, like the previous two, is a moral interpretation of mental retardation.

Walter Rauschenbusch, for instance, believed that this traditional doctrine "was right in emphasizing the biological transmission of evil on the basis of race solidarity," although he rejected the historicity of Adam.

Depravity of will and corruption of nature are transmitted wherever life itself is transmitted. . . . Evil does flow down the generations through

the channels of biological coherence. Idiocy and feeblemindedness, neurotic disturbances, weakness of inhibition, perverse desires, stubbornness
and antisocial impulses in children must have had their adequate biological causes somewhere back on the line, even if we lack the records.[6]

Rauschenbusch used this argument to explain the social nature of
evil. Other less able and sensitive ministers cruelly relate this doctrine to personal misfortune, such as the minister who recently de-
clared from his pulpit that a mentally retarded child was the result
of a "bad seed."

The emotional impact of mental retardation often causes parents
to feel that they are "defective" themselves because they have produced a defective child. Parental anxiety, however, is often relieved
by a simple medical explanation of the cause from a trusted physician. The pastor, therefore, counters this false theological interpretation by assisting the family to secure an accurate diagnosis of the
child's condition.

In disavowing these theological explanations, we have not discounted the relevance of the Christian world view for our understanding of mental retardation. But we have challenged some of
the religious solutions offered for the causation as being "poor"
theology and contrary to the best understanding of mental retardation.

Sense of personal responsibility and guilt.—The theological dimensions of mental retardation are further evident in the parents'
sense of personal responsibility and guilt. Parents often seek to
determine their degree of responsibility for the retarded condition
and the extent to which they are responsible for the care of the child.
In this quest, religious beliefs may either help or hinder. Religious
faith which enables parents to meet the demands of the situation
in a realistic and healthy manner is a constructive force. But religious beliefs used to sustain groundless hopes or to justify the
idolatrous worship of a retarded child are destructive and harmful.
Careful distinctions must be drawn between the family's use and
misuse of religion.

This is particularly necessary with regard to guilt—a common
parental response to the birth of a retarded child. A clear distinction, for instance, is needed between what may be described as
vague guilt feelings and guilt feelings arising from events for which
the parents are actually responsible. In the case of Mr. Tucker, a
vague sense of guilt and unworthiness caused him to attribute his

son's retardation to God's judgment upon his lack of Christian commitment, though he cannot specify acts which make him responsible. However, parental guilt is not always distorted. Some parents are partly responsible for the retardation or for creating conditions which cause retardation.

A sense of guilt is often evident in the parents' attempt to make atonement through overprotection of the child or other compensating tactics. A minister found this to be true of Mrs. Smith, the mother of a three-year-old retarded son. After the minister had inquired about Mrs. Smith's family and religious affiliation, Mrs. Smith disclosed her sense of guilt by declaring that she does not know why God is punishing her. She has searched but cannot find the answer. After briefly exploring her understanding of the nature of God, the minister found that other factors were involved. Following the birth of a daughter, Mrs. Smith had a miscarriage. Although she did not want more children, she soon became pregnant with Sammy. When she began hemorrhaging and was told to go to bed, she deliberately disobeyed the doctor's orders and remained on her feet, trying to cause another miscarriage.

When Sammy was born, however, Mrs. Smith "fell in love with him" because he was so beautiful. She even wished for him to remain her baby forever. She soon forgot this wish but maintained the close relationship with Sammy, although he did not develop as her other child had. When Sammy was two years old, she remarked to Mr. Smith that Sammy still seemed like a baby. She then recalled her former wish. Now she cannot understand why God granted such a wish.

Mrs. Smith's feelings of guilt resulted in an overprotectiveness of Sammy and a withdrawal of attention from her other child and her husband, who now resent the retarded child. Mrs. Smith showers all of her affection and love on Sammy and permits no one else, not even Mr. Smith, to care for him. Consequently, she is so tired at the end of the day that she has no desire even to kiss her husband. She seems to understand her overprotectiveness and the reasons for it, but is inwardly compelled to continue.

What appears to be extreme devotion and love is actually an attempt to atone for the guilt of not wanting the child in the first place, of trying to abort through reversal of the doctor's orders, of the wish for Sammy to remain a baby, and finally, of having displeased God.

Similarly, an elderly mother wore herself out physically and emotionally caring for a severely retarded son. In spite of the admonitions of her family, friends, and physician, the thought of committing the son to an institution overwhelmed her with guilt. Finally, in desperation, she attempted to take her own life, which necessitated the institutionalization of both her and her son. Unresolved guilt resulted in an unrealistic and unhealthy sense of responsibility.

A sense of guilt may motivate parents to make atonement for their imaginary or real failure through the excessive care of the retarded child and the neglect of the other spouse and siblings. It may also drive them to "play God" in that they feel no one else can care for the child as adequately as they.

How parents understand the sovereignty of God may also contribute to unrealistic management of the retarded child. Parents who attribute the retardation to an act of God may continue to believe that God will magically "cure" their child. Mr. Tucker, after living with a retarded son for six years, said: "I haven't given up all hope. If it is God's will, he can heal him. I've sent Junior's name to Oral Roberts for prayer." As with Mr. Tucker, such beliefs often result in an unwillingness to accept the obvious limitations of the child, to realistically integrate him into the life of the family, and to make long-range plans for his lifetime care.

Moreover, parents who believe that God gave them this child may adopt a martyr or "chosen people" complex. They reason that since God gave them this child, they are obligated to do as much as possible for the child. Extreme devotion and care are then heaped upon the defective child, while the needs of other siblings and family members are ignored.

Religious beliefs thus may be "employed in a negative way, delaying realistic, practical action in the immediate present."[7] An unresolved sense of guilt or conviction that God has given them this child may result in overprotection or an idolatrous worship of the child. The pastor, therefore, should gently but firmly challenge the pathological and destructive misuse of religion. He may need to remind the family that the proper object of worship is God, not the retarded child. The health and well-being of the other family members are not to be sacrificed at any cost.

Effect on the religious faith of the parents.—Religious beliefs, we have seen, are dynamically involved in the parental response to the birth of a retarded child and the consequent care which the child requires. On the other hand, emotional forces such as guilt, resentment, bewilderment, and hostility, which beset parents of retarded children, also affect their religious faith.

A final theological dimension requiring pastoral attention is the effect of the birth of a retarded child on the religious faith of parents. Since no research exists regarding this aspect of mental retardation, the following discussion is of necessity based on the empirical observations and "hunches" of pastors and this writer. Some suggestions regarding this effect were reported in the survey of ministers previously mentioned.[8] This study disclosed that the birth of a retarded child had either a positive or negative effect on religious faith or in some cases made no difference whatever. Forty-one per cent of the clergymen reported that a retarded child stimulated greater faith in the parents known to them. One pastor observed that the retardation caused a family to mature in its attitudes toward many things.

Another minister reported that one family's guilt and questions concerning the goodness of God led them to the church seeking an answer. However, 15 per cent believed that having a retarded child had caused doubt about the goodness of God in the parents known to them, while 13 per cent reported that the birth of a retarded child created guilt in other parents. Some of the ministers reported having observed various "ups and downs" in the faith, while others noted that some parents attained a positive religious response only after a struggle. Other respondents observed completely negative religious responses, such as bewilderment and resentment.

The crisis of mental retardation may shatter the belief in a good and merciful God or confirm the nagging suspicion that God is a vengeful judge, visiting punishment for real or imagined sins. With other parents, the same crisis may be the means of discovering that God is the ultimate resource in time of trouble, to be worshiped for what he is in himself, not for his material benefits. But as in other bereavement situations, deep emotions are expressed and ultimate questions are raised before a final solution is achieved, if ever. The difference between the achievement of acceptance and faith or resentment and doubt may be the pastor's sensitivity to the religious concerns raised by mental retardation and his willingness to be a fellow pilgrim with the parents as together they explore the hidden purposes of God.

The Need for Fellowship and Support

Opportunities to minister are not exhausted with a single interview or visit in the home. Mental retardation is a problem of long
duration, and both the continuing care of the child and the religious concerns of the parents require long-term pastoral care.
Thus, the pastoral care of the parents of retarded persons also
involves a ministry of sustaining and support through the fellowship of the church. The church remembers and stands by the family
through both organized and informal services.

When a minister met the Johnsons, parents of a six-year-old
retarded daughter, he found at least two areas where a ministry
of fellowship and support was needed. One was the need for participation in the life of the church. The Johnsons had not attended
church since their retarded daughter was born because of her
severe retardation and unpredictable behavior. They knew of no
church that had classes for the retarded, so they simply stayed
home with her. Another need was for enduring and open relationships with friends to combat their social isolation. For instance,
friends would visit in the home once or twice and then did not
return. Mr. Johnson felt that they were simply curious to find out
what a retarded child is like, and once their curiosity was satisfied,
they withdrew.

What can the church and minister do to meet the parents' need
for fellowship and support? The unique contribution of the pastor
in the care of parents of retarded persons arises from the nature
of his role as a minister. He has both a durable relationship with
the family and the "right" to take initiative in offering services.

The pastor of Mr. Jones, for example, continued his ministry beyond the visit in the hospital when the baby was born, occasional
calls in the home, and an office interview. The pastor described it:

My relationship with the Jones family has been one of a sustaining
nature. I attempted to provide support to the family, plus printed
materials to help them understand their retarded child, etc. Recently the
father was in my study and borrowed the book *Retarded Children:
God's Children* by Sigurd D. Peterson and found it, as he said, "helpful."
I believe the total support of my family in social contacts with them
in their home, in our home, and at public places has been most helpful
to them. The child is now four years of age and they are finding new
strains upon them. They feel more social isolation now than before.
Our presence with them gives some of the acceptance they need at this
time.

With Mr. Jones, the pastor's ministry, sustained over a four-year period, was simply the continuation of a prior relationship, adapted to meet the special circumstances created by the retarded child. The pastor rightly recognized that what the family needed was not formal counseling but a warm, accepting relationship. With other families, however, the pastor must take the initiative in offering support and counsel, as did the pastor of a large suburban church.

As pastor, I visited in the homes of retarded children and endeavored to be as sympathetic and understanding as possible with the anxious parents of these children. I feel that many times burdened parents are looking for someone who is willing to listen to some of their heartaches, even though a complete solution is not available. As pastor, I sought to encourage the parents of retarded children to be ever mindful of their responsibilities to other children in the family, lest they suffer neglect while the parents are meeting the demands of the retarded.

Parents of retarded children also need to be related to church members other than the pastor and to parents of normal children. To meet this need, one pastor often took other church members with him in his regular visits to a family with a retarded child. This served the double purpose of overcoming the social isolation of the parents and of overcoming the fears and anxieties of church members regarding mental retardation.

The burden which accrues from the care of the retarded magnifies the parents' need for worship and participation in the life of the church. This is the second area in which the church ministers to the parents' need for fellowship and support. This ministry, however, cannot be accomplished apart from the church's provision for the retarded person. When the nursing care required by the severely retarded or the uncontrollable behavior of others prevents either one or both of the parents from attending church, it may be necessary to provide nursing care in the home. When the retarded child can benefit from religious training, a special department or class in the church should be organized.

In making special arrangements for the retarded, the church accomplishes two ends. First, the parents are freed from the care of the retarded child to participate in the church program. A minister of religious education writes that "part of the joy in this work is watching parents of the mentally retarded taking part in the church services again. One parent said: 'This is actually the first time I've been able to attend Sunday school in five years.'" Similarly, a pastor noted, "Our department for these children makes it possible for their parents to attend the other activities in the church and thus have a normal spiritual life for themselves so far as the church program is concerned."

Second, the church concretely demonstrates its acceptance of both the parents and the retarded child. Thus the pastor who described his church's ministry as showing "the parents that the mentally retarded child is not the punishment of God, but is to be accepted as other children," gave living expression to this conviction through the organization of a special department and making it a permanent part of their educational program. The effect on parents, as another minister observed, is that "what the church did for their children seemed to enhance their appreciation for their church."

For effective long-term care of parents, the church, in deed as in word, must be a ministering community. Its serving function is only effected through establishing personal relationships with parents and accepting them into the fellowship of the church.

The church's ministry to the family of the mentally retarded is not significantly different from the ministry to other family problems. Mental retardation is basically a family problem to which the family brings its present resources and pattern of meeting crises. However, the birth of a retarded child does create special problems which necessitates a threefold pastoral ministry. Pastoral care is required in the management of the problems created by the retarded condition, in the clarification of the theological dimensions of mental retardation, and in the family's continuing need for fellowship and support. The ministry to the family is prior to the ministry to retarded persons. Yet, only for purposes of discussion can the ministry to either be considered separately. Ministering to the family ministers to the child, and ministering to the child ministers to the family.

Notes

1. Mrs. Max A. Murray, "Needs of Parents of Mentally Retarded Children," *American Journal of American Deficiency*, May, 1959, p. 1081.
2. Gustaf Aulén, *The Faith of the Christian Church*, trans. Eric H. Wahlstrom (Philadelphia: The Muhlenberg Press, 1961), p. 174.

3. Wayne E. Oates, *The Religious Dimensions of Personality* (New York: Association Press, 1957), p. 77.

4. Dale Evans Rogers, *Angel Unaware* (Westwood, N.J.: Fleming H. Revell Co., 1953), p. 7.

5. Hilmar A. Sieving (ed.), *The Exceptional Child and the Christian Community* (River Forest, Ill.: Lutheran Education Association, 1953), p. 17.

6. Walter Rauschenbusch, *A Theology for the Social Gospel* (Nashville: Abingdon Press, n.d.), p. 58.

7. Michaels and Schucman, *op. cit.*, pp. 569-70.

8. Stubblefield, *op. cit.*, p. 141.

Part Two—Ministry to Retarded Persons

4

The Religious Consciousness
of the Retarded

The church's ministry to mentally retarded persons is no different from its ministry to other persons. Much attention has been directed to the development of Christian education programs. By contrast, other areas of ministry, such as pastoral care and social welfare, have largely been neglected. The church's ministry must be perceived in a broad and comprehensive fashion, using all the resources normally employed in ministering to persons.

At the very center of the religious ministry is the question of the religious consciousness of mentally retarded persons. Doctrinal beliefs and practices regarding eligibility for church membership and participation in the fellowship and ordinances of the church vary according to denominations. All, however, face the question of the degree to which retarded persons can understand what it means to be a Christian and a church member.

Approaches to Religious Consciousness

The religious consciousness of the mentally retarded has been interpreted in several ways. A brief survey of some of these approaches may suggest criteria to be used and pitfalls to be avoided in gauging religious consciousness and responsibility.

One approach denies that the mentally retarded have either religious consciousness or responsibility. Such a judgment is derived from the tacit assumption that the retarded are basically not genuine human beings. They are regarded as being *less* than human or *more* than human.

The definition of the image of God in man or of the nature of

54

religion may be so restricted that the retarded are regarded as non-religious persons. This reflects the view that they are less than human. For example, Emil Brunner contends that the mentally retarded are without the image of God. The *imago dei*, Brunner believes, is basically centered in responsibility, and "it only ceases where true human living ceases—on the borderline of imbecility or madness."[1] Similarly, E. S. Ames in his book on the psychology of religion defines religion as the realization of the highest social values. Of nonreligious persons "one class includes those who lack the mentality or the organization of impulses necessary to enable them to share in the appreciation and effective pursuit of ideals." [2] To be a part of society, he contends, one must be able to enter the experiences of other persons and maintain toward them consistent and dependable relations. Therefore, persons who cannot form "efficient habits, employ memory and foresight, and hold with some tenacity to ideal purposes" cannot be religious. Other theologians, such as Paul Tillich,[3] who equate the image of God with man's rational powers would also deny religious consciousness to the mentally retarded.

The Christian interpretation of the nature of man, however, disavows the equation of any one faculty of man with the image of God or the religious consciousness. As Wayne Oates points out, misconceptions of both personality and religion arise from over-classifying them with one particular aspect of either.[4] Consequently, we must reject the categorical classification of the retarded as non-religious persons because they have not attained a heightened sense of responsibility or a high level of rational powers.

Religious consciousness and responsibility are also unwittingly denied by persons who stereotype the retarded as more than human. For instance, the retarded are sometimes considered to be "eternal children," thus classified as children who never develop interests beyond those of a child. This ignores their social development and interest which in many cases parallels that of their normal peers. The retarded are also stereotyped as "heaven's very special children"—the instruments of God for a special mission. While this perspective is fostered by some parents and parent organizations, a similar view is reflected in the attitudes of some religious workers with the retarded. In a conference on "The Church's Ministry in Mental Retardation," a few of the participants extolled the virtues of retarded children by stating that they were all so lovable and a delight to teach. In another context, a minister stated that the retarded may have more right than many normal persons to become members of the church, because they are less guilty of sin. Catholic religious workers with the retarded consistently speak of them as the "Holy Innocents."

The peril of this stereotype is that the basic human nature of the retarded is ignored. In reaction to the belief that the retarded are less than persons, the present emphasis moves too far in the opposite direction. A corrective was desperately needed to counter the belief that the retarded were less than human. Nothing, however, is to be gained through a sentimentality that glosses over the basic humanity of retarded persons.

A second approach concedes religious consciousness to the retarded but subtly denies religious responsibility. Although it is recognized that retarded persons have interest in, and awareness of, religious matters, religious commitments are not seriously honored.

The Hutterite community, for instance, considers the mentally retarded not to be morally responsible for what they do. The community keeps them in line by watching them carefully and punishing those who engage in antisocial activities only if they show sufficient insight to be affected. In *Culture and Mental Disorder: A Comparative Study of the Hutterites and Other Populations*, J. W. Eaton and R. J. Weil report: "In two cases where mildly defective individuals violated a number of religious rules, the community 'cancelled their baptism' rather than excommunicate them. By cancellation of their baptism they were reduced to the status of children, who are thought to be incapable of sinning and therefore can attain salvation automatically."[5]

Similarly, a church member excused the behavior of two retarded adolescents observed kissing each other during the church service by saying that "they are not responsible." However, only a few weeks previously she had voted, along with the rest of the church, to approve these two as candidates for believers' baptism. In reality, these retardates are still considered to be children, not responsible persons. What seems to be lacking in this perspective is a clear understanding of the *degree* of responsibility which retarded persons can assume. Even children are not treated as totally irresponsible persons.

A third approach attributes both religious consciousness and responsibility to the retarded. This view is most clearly upheld by the Lutherans. The strength of this position is the consistent manner in which Lutheran theology regarding sin and redemption is applied to mentally retarded persons. Its weakness, however, results from the failure to accurately and empirically assess the ability of the retarded to understand and appropriate the theological beliefs taught.

The Lutheran position is based on the belief "that nowhere does the Word of God excuse the exceptional child from the guilt of original or inherited sin, which is the total corruption of the human race. Like all infants, the exceptional child needs a Saviour from sin."[6] Although baptism is the means whereby infants are regenerated and brought to faith, the child, at the earliest possible age, "is to be led to a conscious faith in Jesus, his Saviour, and the parents are to teach and train him diligently so that he may live a holy life as a child of God and be saved eternally."[7] Teachers are exhorted to tell every class that Jesus loves every child. "Formally and informally they can be told that Jesus loves children so much that He died on the cross to save them."[8] However, it appears to this writer that too much emphasis is placed on the intellectual content of the Christian faith. Theological concepts are introduced before the retarded child is ready for them. Religious faith should be communicated first through the "language of relationships" and second through the "language of words."

A fourth approach recognizes that religious consciousness and responsibility are relative to mental and chronological development. The limitations of the retarded are realistically accepted, and they are thus judged on the basis of their knowledge and motivation. This perspective avoids the principal errors of the previous three approaches, which show a tendency to pronounce categorical judgments without personal involvement with the retarded and the absolutization of religious responsibility.

How such an approach works out in actual practice is excellently demonstrated in the Lutheran procedure of confirming retarded persons. In a recent conference, specific Lutheran beliefs and practices regarding confirmation were applied as criteria to be used in gauging the readiness of retarded persons to be confirmed. It was agreed that only those who were ready to be communicant members should be confirmed. To be eligible to receive the Lord's Supper, the individual must have been baptized, must be a believer in Christ and capable of examining himself.

Four elements are involved in self-examination: a knowledge of sin, a knowledge of the Saviour, a desire to live a Christian life, and knowledge of what one receives in the sacrament. Only retardates who can fulfil these requirements are to be confirmed. The consensus seemed to be that only "educable" adult retardates were capable of receiving the Lord's Supper, and it was suggested that a retardate should not be enrolled in a confirmation class prior to sixteen years of age. However, some latitude is to be allowed, as Chaplain Strefuert noted. The primary concern of the pastor is "that the retardate through the working of the Holy Spirit has fulfilled the basic scriptural requirements."[9] Any additional requirements must vary with the endowments of the individual. This approach maintains theological integrity while at the same time recognizes the limitations and special needs of the retarded.

The church's understanding of the religious consciousness and responsibility of the mentally retarded determines the nature and extent of its religious ministry. An accurate and realistic understanding, however, cannot be obtained apart from an empirical investigation of at least two facets of the religion of the retarded. These two facets are the levels of religious conceptualization and the meaning of religious experience.

Religious Concepts of the Retarded

The study of the religious concepts of the mentally retarded recognizes the cognitive or intellectual aspects of religion. Such a study is necessary in order to accurately assess the level on which religious training for the retarded must be geared and to determine the religious teachings which they understand. A Sunday school teacher, for example, boasted that some of the members of her "trainable" class could repeat John 3:16, as though this were indicative of their religious knowledge. These persons however, could not even read, much less understand the meaning of "only begotten Son" and other phrases in the verse. A review of the religious conceptualizations of the retarded will be helpful in determining the degree of his religious consciousness.

The general religious concepts of sixty-six institutionalized retarded persons at the Clover Bottom Hospital and School, Donelson, Tennessee, were studied by this writer. These religious concepts were compiled from religious evaluation reports routinely prepared on these residents for diagnostic and disposition clinics. The religious evaluations were grouped and evaluated according to the mental age without consideration for chronological age. However, the subjects ranged in chronological age from six to seventy years—forty-three were adults, twenty were adolescents, and three were preadolescents. Thus, the majority of the subjects had attained their maximum mental development.

Mental age was found to be the most significant factor in the levels of religious conceptualization. As the mental ages of these retardates increased, both the ability to conceptualize religious teachings and the quality of such conceptualization increased. Three distinct levels of religious conceptualization seemed apparent, and these levels roughly corresponded to the three educational categories of "nursing care," "trainable," and "educable."

The quality and number of the religious concepts of the retardates with mental ages below five years (nursing care) were extremely limited. Of the eleven retardates with mental ages in the two-year range, only one conceptualized religious ideas. A fifty-two-year-old woman described God as "God Almighty" and said that he was in heaven with Jesus. Only two of the six retardates in the three-year mental age range were able to conceptualize meaningful religious ideas. A seven-year-old boy with an IQ of 50 conceived of Jesus as a very special man and the Bible as a very special book about God. Of the eight subjects with mental ages in the four-year range, five made meaningful religious conceptualizations. God was conceived of as a human being who cares about everyone and to whom we pray, but no distinction was made between the persons of God and Jesus. The church was identified in terms of its activities: singing, preaching, praying, and reading the Bible. They understood the Bible to be a book about God and Jesus, and identified a Christian as one who is "saved," "a friend of God," and who "goes to heaven when he dies."

As was expected, the religious concepts of the retardates with mental ages of five, six, and seven years (trainable) were more sophisticated in quality and more numerous in quantity than were those of the severely retarded. The concepts were anthropomorphic, concrete, and were apparently learned through previous religious training. There was little ability to conceptualize abstract theological beliefs. In contrast to the previous group, all of these retardates conceptualized religious ideas.

A small percentage believed that God was Spirit, but the majority conceived of God in anthropomorphic terms, such as a person who could heal and help you or as a good man. However, specific ideas regarding the nature of God and his relationship to men were expressed. Two respondents stated that God becomes angry at wrong behavior, particularly at the way people "cuss" and talk. Another person commented that "God is no respecter of persons. He cares for us just as he does for those big men on the outside." It was also said that God helps us and tells us not to "pay any attention to the devil."

Most of these retardates conceptualized of Jesus as a distinct person and described him in terms of his saving work: "one who saves people," "the man who died to save us from sin," and "one who died on the cross." Jesus was also characterized as God's Son and the one who heals people. Most frequently a Christian was defined in relation to certain types of behavior; i.e., a Christian should do right, "live up to God," go to church, pray, and read the Bible. However, some identified a Christian as a church member, one who is baptized, and a believer in Jesus Christ.

In agreement with the concepts of the four-year mental age group, the present group identified the church with certain activities. However, the retardates at the seven-year mental age level consistently used theological concepts to define the church. They identified it as the place where one worships, where one is baptized in the Holy Ghost, and where one "gets religion." Also in contrast to the responses of the lower mental age groups, the retardates at the seven-year level conceptualized of the Bible as a special book, describing it as the "holy" or "good book" and the "Word of God." It was also said that the Bible is "true wherever you read it" and "every word in the Bible is true."

The religious concepts of the retardates at the eight-, nine,- and ten-year mental age levels (educable) tended to be more abstract and theological in nature than those of the "trainable" retardates. With one exception, these respondents conceptualized of God as Spirit. They described God as the "best man in heaven, the one who made the world in six days," and as "the Creator of everything and is everywhere without beginning or end." A more theological understanding of Jesus was also demonstrated at this level of mental development. A thirty-year-old Negro woman stated that Jesus was the Son in the "Father, Son, and Holy Ghost of the Trinity."

Although theological phrases were used to identify a Christian, such as "one who has had his sins taken away" and one who "trusts in the Lord," being a Christian tended to be equated with behavior. In contrast to the trainable group, the educable group demonstrated some knowledge of the meaning of baptism. An elderly Catholic woman defined baptism as a "sacrament which cleanses us of original sin and makes us children of God and inheritors of heaven," while an adolescent retardate, a Baptist, stated that "baptism means you have joined the church of God."

On the basis of this study, three conclusions can be drawn. First, mentally retarded persons at the trainable and educable level consistently conceptualize religious ideas. Second, the quality and number of these religious conceptualizations increase as the mental age increases. Finally, the religious concepts of all retardates tend to be anthropomorphic and related to actual life situations but become more theological and abstract as the mental age increases.

In a more restricted study, the concept of God in the mentally retarded was explored by this writer in collaboration with Mr. Wayne Richards. This study of twenty-two residents of the Clover Bottom Hospital and School sought to determine whether the retarded conceived of God as anthropomorphic (having human characteristics), whether they felt that God was involved in their personal lives, and whether they believed that everyone had the same concept of God as they did. The residents were interviewed and administered a questionnaire. For purposes of comparison, the subjects were divided into two groups: trainable and educable. The chronological ages of the trainable group ranged from thirteen years and one month to eighteen years, and the mental ages from five to six and one-half years. These retardates conceived of God as having human characteristics, believed that God was involved in their lives—they could talk with God through prayer, God knew and cared what they did—and thought that everyone they knew had the same concept of God as they did.

The educable group, with chronological ages ranging from sixteen to thirty-seven and one-half years and mental ages from eight to ten years, had significantly different ideas about God. Although both groups gave many of the same responses, differences were evident in the following areas. The educable group conceived of God as having significantly *less* human characteristics, and many thought of God as Spirit and knew that he was different from man. Also, this group believed that God was much more involved in their personal lives. The difference was most evident in the responses concerning talking with God and may have been due to their being more able to participate in religious activities and relate religious practices to their own lives. Moreover, they recognized that other people had ideas about God different from theirs.

Another facet of the religious conceptions of the retarded, in addition to their understanding of God, Jesus, the church, and the Christian life, is the knowledge of the Bible. The retardates' understanding of the Bible was studied by Chaplain Howard Parshall,[10] through the administration of a Bible knowledge questionnaire to 153 institutionalized mentally retarded persons. The questionnaire consisted of 25 statements about significant persons and events in the Bible, with nine items from the Old Testament and 16 from the New Testament. To determine the ability of the subjects to answer simple questions, a verbal response test was administered. Of the 153 subjects, 105 failed and were eliminated from the study. Most of these were "trainable" residents with a mean mental age of six years and two months, while the mean mental age of the remaining 48 subjects was eight years and ten months.

For purposes of comparison, the Bible knowledge test was administered to approximately 125 persons in the adjoining community. The mean chronological age of the community participants was twenty-one years and nine months, while the mean chronological age of the retardates was twenty-four years and eight months. The mean number of correct responses for the retardates was 15 and for the normals 19. In the distribution of scores, the normals were concentrated in the upper part of the distribution and the retardates in the lower. There was no appreciable difference between the two groups in the number of correct responses to the "easy" items: "Who made the world?" "Where does Jesus live today?" "How did Jesus feed five thousand people?" Nor was there any difference in the correct response to the most difficult item: "Who preached the sermon on the day of Pentecost?"

One conclusion from these studies should be taken seriously in the church's educational ministry to the retarded. The religious consciousness of mentally retarded persons is relative to their mental age. As their mental age increased, their knowledge of religion increased. Severely retarded persons possessed almost no religious knowledge, while the religious concepts of trainable retardates were anthropomorphic and related to their own interpersonal situations, such as defining a Christian in terms of behavior or the church in terms of activities. However, the higher mental age development of the educable retarded which permitted the attainment of academic skills was reflected in their knowledge of the Bible and more theological understanding of the Christian faith.

We should not ask, therefore, if mentally retarded persons have a religious consciousness or if they are religiously responsible, as though this could be answered categorically. What should be determined, instead, is the *degree* of religious consciousness and responsibility. This, however, cannot be determined by a study of the levels of religious concepts apart from exploring the meaning of religious experience to the mentally retarded.

Religious Experience of the Mentally Retarded

In contrast to the retardate's knowledge of religious concepts which is relative to mental age, the manner in which he *experiences* and *uses* religion is relative to both chronological and mental development. Limited mental development means that religion is related to concrete life situations rather than interpreted theologically or abstractly. But the social and interpersonal concerns to which religion is applied emerges from the developmental or life stage which the retarded have attained. As will be seen later, the religious experiences of a sixteen-year-old retarded girl with a mental age of eight parallels that of a normal adolescent rather than that of a normal eight-year-old. Similarly, religion does not mean the same to an elderly retarded woman approaching death as it does to a normal child with a corresponding mental age.

Recognizing that religious experience is conditioned by the developmental stage, pastors, Sunday school teachers, and other religious workers can more meaningfully and realistically relate the Christian faith to the actual needs and interests of retarded persons. Both religiously and socially, the interests and needs of the mentally retarded change as they move from childhood through puberty into adolescence and later into adulthood. This is particularly true for the educable and higher level trainable. Their development more closely approximates that of their normal peers than does the development of the lower level trainable and severely retarded who may never have any religious interests.

Childhood.—The religious responses of preadolescent retardates are similar to those of normal children, which Allport[11] described as being "wholly social in character," egocentric, and anthropomorphic. Religious teachings are related to social experiences, and religious beliefs reflect the teachings of significant adults in their lives and religious communities. To a large degree, this is true of all the mentally retarded. Consequently, the social and ritualistic qualities of the religious response of retarded children should be accepted as appropriate for that stage of development. Thus, a nine-year-old boy's confusion of the *meaning* of prayer with the *mechanics* of prayer was quite natural: "One prays by bowing his head, closing his eyes, folding his hands, and saying the Lord's Prayer."

These responses, however, often can be utilized as opportunities to teach the deeper meaning of the Christian faith. For instance, during a devotional period in a preadolescent class, the teacher told the group that Jesus watched over them at night. One of the boys quickly spoke up and said: "Yes, but Tommy (the ward attendant) watches over us during the day." God's care could only be understood through the care of an attendant whom they could see and trust. The teacher used this opportunity to explain that God expresses his love and concern for us through persons. Later in the school year, an incident involving twin brothers was used to teach the proper way of worship. While the Lord's Prayer was being said, one twin had his head bowed and eyes closed, but the other twin was looking around the room and thumping his fingers on the table. Danny reached over and slapped Donny on the side of the face and said: "Straighten up. We are having chapel." The teacher's response was that worship involved reverence and right attitudes.

Adolescence.—In contrast to the religious responses of children, adolescent retardates begin to appropriate religious teachings to meet concerns derived from their social experiences as adolescents. The coming of puberty sets loose strong physical and emotional forces which must be integrated into the total personality. As do normal adolescents, retardates develop interest in the opposite sex, must learn to control aggressive impulses in a socially accepted manner, and struggle to achieve independence. Consequently, the religious experience of retarded adolescents may be marked by conflict with authority, inability to control impulses, guilt over behavior, and struggle to be a whole person. Some of these dimensions were evident in the following case study.

Placement in a state institution for an eighteen-year-old girl (MA 8-8, IQ 53) became necessary because of antisocial behavior. While receiving casework treatment in the institution, she expressed her problems in religious categories, such as "becoming a Christian again" and "living for God." Because of these concerns she was referred to the chaplain.

Before commitment to the institution, she was baptized and became a member of the church. While attending church one Sunday night she felt "the Spirit of God" inside her urging her to go forward as the pastor gave the invitation. She did so and was "saved." Sometime after this experience, she began associating with the "wrong crowd," taking God's name in vain, and doing things she shouldn't. She does not feel that she is still a Christian.

Her religious experience was marked by inner conflict, an idea of a punishing God, loneliness, and a positive desire to be a Christian. She wanted "to live for God," but something inside her, which she did not understand, did not want "to live for God." Inner conflict was further noted in a dream which she related. After "taking up" with the wrong crowd, her mother and pastor talked with her about doing right. That night in a dream she saw a sheet in which either God or Jesus was wrapped. The person spoke to her and told her to live right.

The idea of a punishing God apparently resulted from previous religious training. When small, she was told by her mother that God kept a book with everyone's name in it and marked an X by your name when you did wrong. When you were good, God made no mark at all. When you died, you went down below if you had been bad, but if you were good, you went to heaven. After relating this incident, she asked about the punishment of Adam and Eve. When they ate the apple, she said, they were put out of the Garden and punished. In discussing this she felt that although God forgave Adam and Eve after their punishment, her situation was different.

The most significant male figure in her life seemed to be her grandfather, who had spent much time with her in talking and reading the Bible. While home for Christmas two months prior to this interview, she learned that her grandfather had died. Still quite upset, she expressed a need for her grandfather to be alive now to teach her how "to live for God."

A positive desire to be a Christian was expressed through her concern about living for God. In several sessions with the chaplain, she was allowed to express her deeper feelings and was helped to understand the nature of God's forgiveness when one sins. She was then permitted to attend a community church on Sunday night and after six months became a member by transfer of letter from her home church.

The stress of adolescence is not as turbulent for every retardate nor as closely identified with religious concerns as it was for this girl. Yet the religious experience of retarded adolescents, by virtue of their widening social experiences, is more like that of normal adolescents than children. While the ability to understand religious teachings is limited by the mental development, religion is *used* to meet problems arising from their changing social role and self-concept as adolescents.

This quickly became apparent in an experimental Christian education program involving children, adolescents, and adults. As was expected, an activity approach with little emphasis on "content" except for pictures and brief stories proved most effective with the children. With students in early and middle adolescence who were beginning to read, activity and "content" were combined. Because of their ability to read, they were interested in learning about the Bible, particularly the names of the books of the Bible. For students in late adolescence and young adulthood, a discussion method proved effective. Much class time was used in discussing personal problems with the "content" material being related to actual experiences and needs. Older adults responded to a Bible class approach.

Adulthood.—The religious concerns and interests of mentally retarded adults are not significantly different from those of normal adults. Their understanding of the more intellectual and abstract aspects of the Christian faith, of course, is limited. For instance, three Sundays before Christmas in a class of middle-aged, retarded women, the teacher spent the forty-five-minute session discussing the meaning of Christmas. He shared with the group his delight over seeing the beauty of Christmas lights and decorations in a nearby park. They then read the Christmas story from the Gospel of Luke, discussed the meaning of Christmas, and shared their thoughts about this season. Similarly, another teacher took a class of adult women to her home for a Christmas party. The ladies received presents, talked with each other and visitors from the church, and enjoyed the refreshments. At the conclusion of the party, they attended the Sunday evening worship service.

Church membership and participation in the life of the church are particularly important. They are interested in Bible study, church attendance, and social activities associated with the church. They also identify themselves with particular denominations and often attach importance to their religious beliefs.

Establishing a meaningful relationship with the fellowship of believers is only one religious concern. A second concern with obvious religious overtones is the adult retardate's desire to be a useful and contributing member of society. However, many retarded persons are often frustrated in this attempt. A retarded man with some ability was kept at home because of his parents' unwillingness to risk a job placement in the community. Subsequently, the young man became bored, frustrated, and quite angry with his parents. Here the religious issue is the nature of one's response to limitations and the meaning that one discovers within them.

This problem is especially acute for those living in institutions where restrictions on personal freedom are unavoidable. How one responds to this situation is basically a religious decision. It involves acceptance of limited ability and responsibility for using to the fullest the ability one does possess. This became a real crisis for a middle-aged woman, institutionalized since adolescence. Previous job placements in the community were unsuccessful because of her chronic complaints and dissatisfaction. After returning to the institution from an unsuccessful placement, she became quite concerned about the restricted "boundaries" of her life. Now that she was approaching middle age she realized that there would be few opportunities for returning to the community to live. Unfulfilled sexual needs began to reassert themselves. She threatened to run away if a placement could not be found. In the ninth interview, however, she identified the reason for her restlessness and despondency. She realized that if she were to accomplish anything in life outside the institution, she must accomplish it now. But as to the reasons for her behavior, which resulted in the termination of several job placements, she demonstrated little insight; nor did she accept responsibility for changing her behavior.

Mentally retarded adults must also face death. In this writer's observation, the recognition that death is the inevitable end of life presents no threat to the retarded as it does to many normal persons. Death seems to be accepted as a matter-of-fact. A resident once stopped and told me about the death of the mother of a hospital employee. He knew the lady well, having worked in her home on several occasions. In addition to his sense of personal loss, his response was: "God has a place to care for people like that. No one can live forever. We all have to die." Elderly retardates may also view death as a welcome visitor and respond similarly to other older persons. An eighty-three-year-old retarded woman who had been sick all winter expressed the desire to die. Everything was right between her and God and, since she was old and had suffered for a long time, she was ready to go.

What religion means to retarded persons is relative to the developmental stage in life as well as the level of mental ability. While the retarded conceptualize religious ideas similar to children, it is wrong to assume that they experience religion as a child. What religion means to a retarded person depends upon whether he is a child, an adolescent, or an adult.

/ *Concrete expressions of religious experience.*—Limited mental development means that religion is understood and used in concrete ways to meet actual life situations. At all the developmental stages, religious teachings are applied to social, personal, and ethical concerns, though higher level educable retardates tend to understand more abstract theological ideas. These concrete expressions are evident in several aspects of the retarded's response to religion.

First, sin, guilt, and forgiveness are related to specific acts rather than to the whole relationship of man to God or of man to man. For the retarded, sin usually means the violation of rules or commandments for which guilt is felt and forgiveness sought. An adult retardate who "rededicated" her life at a church service said that she felt guilty because she had taken property that belonged to someone else and had said "bad" words. Feeling that she needed forgiveness, she went forward to ask the pastor to pray for her. She had already asked God to forgive her and felt that he had.

Such a concrete understanding of religion often results in the tendency to identify religion with ritualistic and stereotyped practices. To be religious or Christian may simply mean that one attends church, helps others, and abstains from "wrong" behavior. The whole meaning of religion is equated with patterns of behavior and activity. An extreme example is the case of an adult retardate who began to closely follow a radio preacher. Every weekday and Sunday morning he listened to the radio program of this local pastor, who also tended to identify religion with behavior and frequently exhorted the listeners to give up the ways of the world. Among the practices considered to be worldly were ball games, movies, television, and dances. This so impressed the retardate that for more than three years he refused to attend ball games, movies, or watch television, because he considered these to be worldly things unworthy of a Christian.

Religious teachings, however, when flexibly and realistically interpreted, are significant guides for the retarded as they seek to form meaningful relationships with other persons and develop socially accepted patterns of behavior. For instance, in several Sunday morning worship services, I used some of the Ten Commandments as illustrations of right behavior toward our friends. One morning after church, a girl about twelve years of age asked if the reason I preached on "Thou shalt not take the name of the Lord thy God in vain" and "Thou shalt not steal" was because they did those things. I replied that I knew some of them did those things. She laughed and said that sometimes she "cussed," especially when she got mad. The next Sunday before church began she asked if I was going to tell them not to take the Lord's name in vain again. She needed to hear this often because, as she said, "sometimes I forget."

A second area in which religious experience is expressed concretely is the retardate's understanding of the meaning of being a Christian and a church member. When twelve educable adolescent and adult residents of a state school began attending the Training Union and Sunday evening worship service at one of the local Baptist churches, seven of the group became interested in joining the church. The basic motivation for becoming a member of the church seemed to be social. They had developed a very positive feeling for the church and the members and being baptized seemed to be a way of becoming a permanent part of this group.

One boy, for example, believed that everyone should belong to a church, and since he was now old enough to belong, he saw no reason to delay. However, three of the seven verbalized theological reasons, although it was never clear to what degree they understood these. Joining the church, to one girl, meant to repent of your sins; to another, it meant that you wanted to live for God; while one boy said that Christ died for him and would take him to heaven when he died. The ethical dimension of this experience became obvious when they were asked what it meant to be a Christian. Most of the replies indicated that being a Christian was closely related to behavior; i.e., praying every night, doing right, and helping people who need help.

What it means to retarded persons to be accepted into the fellowship of the church, however, is not adequately conveyed by their words. Acceptance and participation in the Christian community and a high sense of moral conduct are significant aspects of the total meaning of religious experience, even if the theological implications are not fully understood. Consequently, when one of these boys experienced severe inner conflict over an impulsive and immature act, he sought the church's support in his efforts to be a better person. During the invitation at the close of a Sunday evening service, he went to the front of the church, shook hands with the pastor, and returned to his pew. He said that he went forward because he wanted to be a better person, and it would help him if people prayed for him. His desire to be a better person stemmed from a recent failure in a community job placement. During the course of his employment, some of the employees thoughtlessly joked about his being from an institution for the retarded and accused him of stealing money. When this harassment became unbearable, he ran off. Now he felt remorse for this impulsive act and desired to be a better person.

Unlike this boy who accepted responsibility for his actions and utilized religious resources in a healthy fashion, some retardates manipulate Christian doctrine and religious symbols to serve their own ends.

A third concrete expression of religious experience is found in the tendency to attribute magical powers to religion. Thus, a high level educable woman reported that she almost had a "spell," but she prayed and it didn't happen because she had the Lord's Prayer (contained in a locket) around her neck.

Often religion becomes a magical means of resolving conflict, both psychic and interpersonal. A thirty-eight-year-old man seized upon the visible symbol of baptism as a means of becoming a good person. His first indication of religious concern was expressed during conversation with the chaplain. Because of his "mooning" at the girls in the dining room, the nursing supervisor asked the chaplain to talk with him. When the resident was confronted with his behavior, he immediately admitted his wrong. He expressed a desire to be right in his heart and to be "saved." At one time he was "saved," but he did not feel "saved" now because of his behavior. When asked if God would forgive his wrongs, he replied that God would if he confessed, got down on his knees, and prayed. A short time later a second incident occurred. He became so angry with another resident that blows were exchanged. When knocked from his wheelchair, on crutches he attempted to escape from the institution. Again, he related this behavior to religious concern. He stated that he often became so angry he did not know what to do. Realizing that this was wrong, he wanted God to forgive him, because this would make him feel good in his heart. He expressed the desire to be baptized and felt that this would help him to be a good boy in the future.

Similarly, a sixteen-year-old girl in the upper "educable" range believed that "being saved" should resolve her interpersonal problems. In reality, "being saved" meant that she could manipulate God as she had her family and friends. While living with an aunt and uncle, she became unmanageable, left the house often without permission, and told untrue tales about her aunt. Other relatives attempted to keep her but were equally unsuccessful. Several jobs were secured, but she was always dismissed because of conflict with the employers. Although she read the Bible daily, prayed, and refused to wear make-up, dance, or attend movies, she was disturbed by her inability to get along with people. Trying to resolve this conflict, she responded to the altar call on several consecutive Sundays. Each time she presented herself at the altar, she felt "saved," but some conflict would arise during the week which caused her to doubt. After several Sundays, she felt assured that she was "saved." However, the pattern of manipulative, hostile behavior continued, resulting in her institutionalization. She confessed faith in God, but related to him in an extractive way, feeling that because God did not get her out of the institution, he no longer cared for her.

The concrete interpretation of religion means that Christian doctrine and biblical teachings must be related to actual experiences rather than being taught abstractly. Theological concepts commonly used and understood by church members need to be reformulated and expressed in simple terms. However, the retardeds' inability to understand the more intellectual aspects of theology does not make the Christian faith less meaningful to them than to normal persons. It simply means that religious experiences and concerns are expressed concretely, in social and ethical terms. With the retarded, as with all persons, the deepest and most profound theological truth—that we are loved and accepted by God through Jesus Christ—is communicated through participation in the life of the church. What one feels and experiences is more important than the depth of his thought.

The nature and extent of the church's ministry is determined by the degree of religious consciousness and responsibility ascribed to the mentally retarded. To assess the degree necessitates the correlation of theological definitions of religious responsibility with empirical studies of religious consciousness, as has been done in this chapter. This study of religious consciousness is an essential foundation. Upon this a sound Christian education program and ministry of pastoral care are based. The following two chapters discuss in detail how such a ministry is effected.

Notes

1. Emil Brunner, *The Christian Doctrine of Creation and Redemption*, trans. Olive Wyon (Philadelphia: The Westminster Press, 1952), p. 57.

2. Edward Scribner Ames, *The Psychology of Religious Experience* (Boston: Houghton Mifflin Co., 1910), pp. 359-60.

3. Paul Tillich, *Systematic Theology* (Chicago: University of Chicago Press, 1951), I, 259.

4. Wayne E. Oates, *op. cit.*, p. 31.

5. J. W. Eaton and R. J. Weil, *Culture and Mental Disorder: A Comparative Study of the Hutterites and Other Populations* (Glencoe, Ill.: The Free Press, 1955), p. 157.

6. Sieving (ed.), *op. cit.*, p. 12.

7. *Providing a Program of Christian Education for the Mentally Retarded* (St. Louis: Board of Parish Education, The Lutheran Church-Missouri Synod), p. 23.

8. *Ibid.*, p. 24.

9. "Selected Presentations of the Institute on the Religious Education of the Mentally Retarded" (Watertown, Wis.: Bethesda Lutheran Home, 1962), p. 7.

10. Howard W. Parshall, "A Bible Knowledge Test for Institutionalized Mental Defectives," *American Journal of Mental Deficiency*, May, 1960, p. 960.

11. Gordon W. Allport, *The Individual and His Religion* (New York: The Macmillan Co., 1960), pp. 28-32.

5

Christian Education
of the Retarded

The Christian education of the mentally retarded is one aspect of the church's total teaching ministry. It is different only in degree, not in kind, from that provided for normal persons.

Consider, for example, a Christian education class for ten trainable retarded children, who are also members of a "sense-training" class in a state institution. All of these children, ranging in age from preadolescence to early adolescence, are toilet-trained and can walk. Some, however, have little or no speech. Except for one lethargic girl, they are active, distractible, and able to concentrate on any one task for only a short period of time. On the tables in their classroom are educational toys designed to teach colors and the different sizes, shapes, and textures. Pupils are permitted to play with any of the toys which attracts their attention. Usually they play alone rather than with each other. After a brief period of play, the teacher reminds them that this is the day the chaplain comes. The teacher then begins to sing a chorus and encourages the children to sing with her. After several brief choruses, the chaplain tells a Bible story in short, simple sentences and with the aid of a teaching picture. A brief prayer follows in which God is thanked for his care, for teachers, and for the food we eat. The children then move to the kitchen where juice and cookies are served. Although little "formal" teaching has taken place, these children know that Monday morning is the time for Sunday school and for their preacher to visit the class.

Compare and contrast this class with one for eight educable retardates in late adolescence. Upon entering the classroom, they sit around a table. The secretary, one of the class members, checks the roll. An informal discussion follows in which each person is encouraged to share any significant event of the previous week.

The teacher introduces the lesson by observing that almost every week we are faced with new situations and tasks. Sometimes when we face strange experiences we are afraid. This is what happened to Simon Peter on the night that Jesus was arrested. Does anyone know where this story is found in the Bible? Since no one knows, the teacher opens the Bible to the Gospel of Luke. After the story is told, the students are involved through the use of questions regarding the reasons for Peter's fear, what he did because he was afraid, and how Jesus dealt with him. The story is then related to their personal experiences. They, too, have been afraid. One is afraid of the dark, while another is afraid that he cannot learn all that is expected of him in school. The teacher then guides the students to describe their reaction to fear and how they can meet and overcome their fears.

Following the story and discussion, the Bible verse is presented in the form of a puzzle. The students put the puzzle together and then read the Bible verse. The teacher writes it on the board, the class repeats it, and its meaning is discussed and related to the lesson and to their lives. The concerns presented in the class are brought together in the final ten minutes of the class. Two hymns, selected by the students, are sung, and the teacher briefly summarizes the lesson and discussion. The students are asked to suggest concerns to be included in the prayer. Each student is encouraged to pray openly. The teacher himself prays and then guides the students in repeating the Lord's Prayer.

This description of two classes illustrates the problem involved in programing Christian education for retarded persons. Basically the problem stems from the inability of the retarded to benefit from Christian education appropriate for their chronological age. For instance, the approach used with the trainable class corresponded in many respects with a nursery or kindergarten class, while the lesson used with the educable class was loosely adapted from Primary-age material. Yet the educable adolescents are certainly not Primaries, either in physical size or social interest. This disparity between chronological age and mental functioning raises questions regarding the nature and purpose of Christian education and approaches to be used at the various levels of retardation. A practical question concerns the methods and procedures to be used in providing religious training for retardates in the local church. Questions are also asked about the qualification and function of the religious teacher of the retarded.

The purpose of the present chapter, therefore, is to suggest a philosophy of Christian education for the retarded, some principles for organizing and structuring a program in the local church, and the training and role of the teachers.

Philosophy of Christian Education

The soundness of the religious training provided for the mentally retarded hinges upon the soundness of the undergirding philosophy. The growing interest in Christian education for the retarded has not resulted in nor grown out of a sound philosophy. Rather, the interest has focused on methods and techniques of teaching. A general philosophy is urgently needed. A comprehensive Christian education program, which is guided by sound principles, includes at least three elements.

Relation to general Christian education.—There is but one philosophy of Christian education for both "retardates" and "normals." Christian education of the mentally retarded is different only in degree, not in kind. Failure to appreciate this has resulted in misconceptions of Christian education for the retarded. These misconceptions are most evident in attempts that have been made to develop curriculum materials.

In one approach to curriculum development, the dominating concern is to teach the Bible and theological doctrine. As part of a unit prepared for young children, lessons are included on the creation, the fall of man, and the ascension of Jesus, with much emphasis on "being saved." Another example of this approach is found in a series of lessons designed for use with "trainable" children. Pictures were used depicting the Fall, showing Eve being tempted by the serpent, plucking the apple off the tree, eating it, and persuading Adam to eat. The final picture shows God forcing Adam and Eve from the Garden, for they had disobeyed. The moral is that "we must obey."

A second approach treats Christian education as character education, with a resulting emphasis on behavior or attitudes. Akin to this is a third approach, which regards Christian education for the retarded as social experience, with the nature of the "content" considered unimportant.

Each approach embraces essential elements of Christian education, but every one suffers from an overemphasis on one dimension. The emphasis on theological content fails to appreciate both the religious development and the religious need of retarded persons. The emphasis on character education obscures the nature of Christian education by using religion to foster certain behavior patterns. The emphasis on social experience discounts the purpose of Christian education and the interest of retarded persons in religious knowledge.

A second misconception is evident in the formulation of the objective of Christian education. In recognizing the limited development of the retarded, some persons believe it necessary to formulate special objectives to be accomplished in the Christian education of the retarded. In a conference of state school chaplains,[1] eight objectives were suggested. These objectives were both religious and social. The religious objectives included developing the "God consciousness," understanding Jesus as a friend, participation in worship, and appreciation of the Bible. The social goals related to the retardates' character formation, contribution to society, and participation in their primary social group. The danger of this approach, however, is that no one objective controls the development of curriculum materials, nor does it recognize that the retardates do not comprise a homogeneous group.

A more feasible approach is the acceptance of the general objective of Christian education as the basic objective of Christian education for the retarded and the development of curriculum materials appropriate to the level of sociointellectual development, as is done with specific age groups. The problem then becomes one of determining the degree to which the objective of Christian education can be attained with retardates at the various educational and developmental levels. Thus, the basic principles regarding the scope, purpose, process, and design of Christian education for normal persons would be the guidelines for developing a Christian education program for mentally retarded persons.

Religious development.—Christian education must be geared to the development of the retarded. The task then is to plot a sequence of religious development according to both the educational and developmental level. Both mental and social maturity as measured by mental age and chronological age must be considered. Mental maturity is the clue to gauging the difficulty of material which the retarded can understand, while social maturity is the clue to the way retardates experience religion and appropriate it for personal ends.

Previous illustrations have shown the importance of considering both mental and chronological age. If only one measurement of maturity, such as mental age, had been used with the retardates in the educable class using Primary material, the content of the material would have been geared for children. The social interests of these persons, however, are more like those of normal adolescents than Primary children. Applying the biblical story to the interests of children would have completely missed the needs of these adolescents. Therefore, to determine the difficulty of material to be presented, the mental age of the retarded should be correlated with the corresponding developmental level of normal children. In providing experiences to make the gospel meaningful and relevant to actual needs, social maturity is the guide.

As a framework for charting the religious development, the educational classification of nursing care, trainable, and educable will be used.

Retardates at the lowest level of mental and social functioning are considered to be a medical and nursing problem rather than an educational one. Although some motor and speech development may occur, retardates at this level cannot benefit from training in self-help skills; they are totally incapable of self-maintenance and require complete nursing care. At a more advanced chronological age, some may find pleasure in pictures, stories, and music, but they are unable to understand the gospel in relation to their own lives. They cannot profit from structured religious training. The only direct religious ministry the church may provide is nursing care, either at the church or in the home, so that the parents may participate in the activities of the church.

At the moderate level of retardation religious training is possible; but, since the developmental rate is considerably slower than normal, a special program is required. The developmental rate of trainable retardates is from one-fourth to one-half of a year in any one calendar year, and the IQ ranges from 30 to 50. In determining methods, religious understanding, and religious responsibility, one must use the developmental level as the basic guideline.

Christian education for preadolescents, for example, should be geared at the nursery or kindergarten level. At six years of age their mental development is on the level of a year and a half- to three-year-old child and at nine years on a two and a half- to four and a half-year level. For trainable adolescents, material geared at the kindergarten or Primary level is appropriate, since at twelve years they function on a three- to six-year level and at maturity on a four- to eight-year level. However, as the retardates in the upper range of the trainable classification mature chronologically, their social interest approximates that of their normal peers. Since adolescents realize that they are not children, the material and activities should be geared to both mental and social maturity and should be made relevant to social experience. For children the story of Jesus in the Temple may simply illustrate that Jesus went to church, but for adolescents it illustrates Jesus' relation to authority—a real problem for many of them.

The religious concepts of the moderately retarded, even in adulthood, are those of children. As previously noted, God is conceived of as a human being; Jesus is regarded as a human being with special qualities; a Christian is identified in relation to stereotyped behavior; and the Bible is a good book that tells us about God and Jesus. Biblical stories, such as the fall of Adam, the transfiguration, or the ascension of Jesus, are not appropriate for this group, even when told in simple language. The teachings of the gospel are relevant only in relation to concrete situations, not as abstract principles or eternal truths. Since abstract thinking is impossible at this level of mental functioning, the emphasis of the class is centered around social experiences, and the gospel is applied to these.

Limited mental development and religious knowledge renders most trainable retardates incapable of making a responsible religious decision regarding their relationship to Jesus Christ. They apply religious teachings to actual life situations involving attitudes, interpersonal relationships, and behavior. Such understanding does not constitute knowledge of sin against God and redemption through Jesus Christ. Consequently, evangelism should not be an objective of Christian education for the moderately retarded.

Thus, the Christian education of trainable retardates presents a distinct problem. Their religious development will not exceed that of a Primary child; and, in most cases, they will never become participating members of the church. However, most of them benefit from religious training, which can only be accomplished through special classes, apart from classes for the normal children.

With the educable the problem is similar but somewhat different. Although the mental and social development of the mildly retarded more closely approximates normal development, the differences in levels of development are significant enough to warrant special consideration. For instance, the developmental rate of educable retardates is one-half to three-fourths of a year in any one calendar year. Their maximum mental development will not exceed eight to twelve years, while the IQ range is between 50 and 75.

Such disparity between mental age and chronological age necessitates an adjustment in the level at which education is geared. Educable retardates between six and ten years with mental ages from three to six and a half benefit from religious training on a kindergarten or beginning Primary level. Preadolescents, ten to twelve, with mental ages from six and a half to nine years, can handle material on a Primary level, while advanced Primary or Junior material is appropriate for adolescents. However, the content of the material must be geared to their social maturity. Adolescents, for example, are striving for independence, forming relations with persons of the opposite sex, learning vocational skills, and assuming new roles at home and in the school and community.

The religious knowledge of educable retardates is more advanced than that of the trainable group but less advanced than that of normal persons. For example, educables can conceive of God as a Spirit. They can identify Jesus as the Son of God and as the Saviour. The Bible is recognized as a holy book, written by different authors and at different times. Also, the mildly retarded can read the Bible for themselves and learn some of its content. A Christian is still identified with certain patterns of behavior, but many retardates relate being a Christian to trust in God, forgiveness of sin, baptism, and church membership. Though the religious concepts are more abstract and theological in nature than those of the trainable, the religious concepts of the mildly retarded still tend to be concrete and are related to actual life situations rather than understood as independent intellectual ideas.

Most educable retardates in late adolescence are ready to be considered for church membership either through baptism or confirmation, depending upon church polity. With careful instruction, they can understand what it means to be a Christian and a church member. For this to be a meaningful experience, the church must exercise patience and responsibility. With these persons, Christian nurture is the best form of evangelism, since they have neither the emotional nor the mental ability to make much sense of an emphasis on conversion.

Thus, proper appreciation for the religious development will insure Christian education appropriate for the level of mental and social maturity. This frees the retarded from unrealistic expectations of anxious religious workers who demand either too little or too much.

Religious needs.—Christian education may be geared to the level of religious development and still appear as something imposed upon retarded persons because it does not meet felt religious concerns. Christian education must be relevant to the retardate's religious needs. His needs are no different in kind from the needs of normal persons, but his limited mental development attaches extreme importance to two factors—involvement in the church and interpersonal relationships.

The importance of the church as the mediating agency of the gospel is magnified. The retarded's inability to understand abstractions necessitates a concrete approach. For him, involvement in the church as an accepting community is the heart of Christian education. Through participation in its life, he is introduced to the church's teachings, worship, sacraments, and fellowship.

As Miller says: "Christian education is what happens to a person within a Christian community."[2] What happens depends upon the mental and chronological age of the individual and the response of the church. For children, the church may mean nothing more than a friendly place associated with Sunday, music, the Bible, and good times with other children. For example, a retarded child was a complete misfit every place he went in the church until a special department was created for him. After a happy experience one Sunday, the next Sunday he woke up saying: "Go to Sunday school, go to Sunday school."

Even for severely retarded adults, the church may become a meaningful community. An adult man in a rural community found it so. Although he could not speak understandably, he developed a strong attachment for the church and the minister. He attended church every Sunday, though it is doubtful that he ever understood the sermon. The church members, as well as the minister, warmly accepted this man into their fellowship. Thus the church became the center of meaning in his life.

For educable adolescents and adults, the church has deeper meanings. They desire to be accepted as members and to participate in the worship and social life. However, the church can also drive retarded persons away. A retarded adolescent attended Sunday school one Sunday morning. He never came back because some of the class members made fun of his clothes.

The meaningfulness of Christian education is conditioned by the context in which it occurs. Even when formal religious training is impossible, the compassion of Christ can be communicated through the compassion of the church. On the other hand, attitudes of rejection are also communicated. How the church *feels* toward retarded persons counts far more than what the church *says*.

It is important that the Christian faith be communicated as "story," as events and persons, with the dynamic qualities and interpersonal aspects related to actual life situations. The Christian faith is most relevant to the lives of retarded persons when applied to their total range of relationships. Although what the gospel means varies according to the educational and developmental level, religious teachings are applicable to personal and interpersonal relationships.

The gospel communicates a "feeling tone," and the importance of this should not be underestimated. Sigurd D. Petersen in *Retarded Children: God's Children*[3] relates the gospel to three personal needs of retarded persons. Because of their history of failure and rejection, the retarded need to identify with the good things of life. These are communicated through such concepts as God, Jesus, prayer, love, friends, and the world of nature. Emotional needs for love and assurance that they are important, wanted, and accepted are met through such concepts as love, faith, hope, forgiveness, trust, meaning of life, personal worth, the cross of Christ, and the resurrection. The need for self-control and restraint is communicated through such concepts as the Ten Commandments, obedience, right and wrong relationships, the will of God, and responsibility.

One need of the retarded is to learn right ways of relating to peers and authority persons. For example, retarded children need to be taught to share the toys in the classroom and not hit other class members. Older retardates need to learn to "talk out" negative feelings of anger and frustration instead of acting them out. For the mildly retarded, the development of right relations with persons of the opposite sex is a definite problem. Since many of these persons marry, the teacher or minister, at an appropriate time, should frankly and forthrightly interpret to older adolescents and adults the Christian view of sex and marriage. Retarded persons can understand that sexual intercourse is reserved for married persons since children may result who need parents to care for them.

Retarded persons have contact with "communities" such as the church, the home, the school, and businesses. They are not to be treated as irresponsible persons. Rather, they should be expected to contribute constructively to the community or institution in which they live. Responsible behavior for children may mean nothing more than picking up their playthings in Sunday school, while older retardates could be responsible for arranging the chairs in the room. Assumption of responsibility appropriate for the level of development is a Christian teaching. This can be presented biblically through the parable of the talents which clearly teaches Jesus' desire that we be trustworthy in whatever is assigned to us.

Retarded persons need to be rightly related to God. Like all other persons, the retarded need to have life set in the context of God's providence, love, and concern. However, religion is often misinterpreted to them. In extensive contact with institutionalized retardates, it is quite obvious that religion is usually used to control behavior. Their religious conversation reflects much about God's expectations of them but reflects little understanding of forgiveness and acceptance. Conversely, retarded persons themselves often misinterpret religious teachings. Understanding prayer as a magical device, they may often ask their pastor to pray for their mother to get well, for visits from the family, or for money. In relating retarded persons to God, both "law" and "gospel" are important, as well as clear teachings regarding God's usual way of relating to us.

All three elements—the integral relation to general Christian education, awareness of the level of religious development, and appreciation for the religious needs—are essential in the development of a sound philosophy of Christian education for the mentally retarded. By maintaining these three perspectives, attempts to religiously train retarded persons will be attempts at Christian education relevant to the sociointellectual development and to the total range of relationships to which the teachings of the gospel are applicable.

Organizing and Structuring a Local Church Program

Effective Christian education for retarded persons depends upon the organization and structure of the program. In beginning such a ministry, churches commonly confront at least three problems. These problems involve the relation of the special program to the total church program, the management of retarded persons in existing programs, and the creation or organization of a special class or department.

Relation to total church program.—The Christian education of the mentally retarded should be integrally related to the educational ministry of the church. Since the church's work with the retarded is relatively new, many church members are understandably cautious in committing the church to this ministry. Christian education classes are often regarded as special programs for which the church provides a room and equipment but exercises little control over the enrolment of pupils or selection of the teachers.

Ideally the church itself takes the initiative to meet the special needs of the retarded persons within its fellowship and/or in the general community. If the pastor, education director, and Sunday school teachers maintain contact with parents and children, they readily know of any children with special needs. Once these are known, steps can be taken to provide appropriate religious training. A minister of education described the procedure followed in his church: "Our efforts in this area of teaching have succeeded because our pastor has given total support to the program. This, along with general churchwide support, is vital. Dr. G. and I discussed this work thoroughly before any public mention was made. We then sought advice and assistance from professional educators on methods and materials. Fortunately, our church people have accepted the challenge and have given solid support." This successful program was characterized by progressive and committed leadership, careful planning along with consultation from professional persons, and recognition that this ministry involved the whole church.

In some situations, however, the initiative is taken by the parents or interested friends. The program then tends to be dominated by a few persons rather than under control of the church. For example, one church became interested in providing a special class through the efforts of a mother with a retarded child. She tacitly assumed that she would be the teacher and began recruiting other retarded children whose parents were not members of the church. Furthermore, she expected the church to furnish a room, equipment, materials, and other teachers. The church endorsed the proposed program but did not assume responsibility for its implementation. Rather, it was assumed that the mother and pastor would formulate specific policy and secure the necessary resources. The mother though tended to assume the responsibility. Consequently, the pastor was caught between an aggressive mother and an irresponsible church.

To avoid what can develop into a serious church problem, clear administrative responsibility should be fixed in the education director, the Sunday school superintendent, or the Christian Education Committee. They in turn survey the needs, the church resources, the number of pupils to be enrolled, and make recommendations to the whole church for endorsement. Without establishing clear responsibility and limits, the church may overextend itself, beginning a program for which the church has neither the resources nor the ability to effectively maintain. We can be no less responsible in ministering to the mentally retarded than we are in ministering to other persons.

In summary then, a responsible ministry includes the following procedures: (1) the program for the retarded is viewed as one aspect of the total church program, the church establishing policy and regulations; (2) an accurate survey is made of the number of retarded children, including the degree of retardation if available; (3) the resources of the church are ascertained as to available space, teachers, and the number of children for whom adequate provision can be made; (4) the parents of these children are visited, informed personally of the church's intentions, and their support is enlisted— the parents themselves may have some embarrassment regarding the identification of their child as retarded; and (5) professional persons, when available, are enlisted to acquaint the church with the needs of the retarded and to train the teachers.

II   *Management of retarded persons in existing programs.*—In meeting the special needs of the retarded, two courses of action are open. One possibility, of course, is the creation of a special department or classes. Some guidelines for such a program will be discussed later. However, in many churches the retarded are integrated into existing classes or are taught individually.

The principle reasons for excluding a retarded person from his regular class are his inability to keep up with the other children or because his presence disrupts the class. With special attention, young children and older high-level educable retardates often are able to remain in their regular class. As one pastor reports: "So far, our children are in with normal children and doing all right. They are under observation and changes will be made as needed." Similarly, another pastor says: "We have a graded Nursery and Sunday school which helps in placing them in areas where they can keep up." In one church a girl, small for her age, was kept with a class two years below her chronological age. She enjoyed the class, participated in its activities, and seemed to be well accepted by the other girls. Although not always an ideal arrangement, this may be the most feasible approach when there may be only one or two retarded children in the church.

Development of special classes.—When retarded persons, for various reasons, cannot be integrated into a regular class, special arrangements are necessary. In one instance, a church with two ten-year-old retarded children taught them separately, using curriculum material designed for four-year-olds with one and material for two-year-olds with the other. In large churches with several retarded persons or when the church is willing to include other children from the community, special departments or classes in the Sunday school may be organized. The retarded persons then are taught in separate classes.

Although many churches are currently providing special religious education classes, the principles for organizing and structuring such classes and selecting methods and materials for teaching are not well developed. In this respect Christian education for the retarded is in the pioneer stage, often lagging far behind the best practice of general Christian education. Successful management and training of the mentally retarded in special Christian education classes depends upon the organization, structure, and methods. This we know is important in the religious training of normal children, and it is no less important with the retarded.

In organizing a special class, the first step is to secure a homogeneous organization. With the retarded, as well as the normal person, some form of grading must be utilized. Previous discussions have effectively demonstrated that the mentally retarded do not comprise a homogeneous group. For example, all of the retardates in both the "trainable" and "educable" classes mentioned at the first of the chapter require special classes, but they do not need to be in the same class. There is too much difference between their intellectual ability and social interest. Moreover, consider a class with three ten-year-old boys, all obviously retarded. One is severely retarded, makes no meaningful communication, is unresponsive to other persons, and is not toilet-trained. Another has some speech, participates in group activities if supervised, but possesses no academic skills whatever. The third boy, however, is beginning to count, write, and read on a first-grade level. While none of the boys can profit from religious training appropriate for their chronological age, neither should they be grouped together. They are all ten years old, but they function on quite different levels.

Even the highest level trainable retardates in late adolescence and adulthood realize that they are not children. One such boy, given a Nursery pamphlet in Sunday school, was quite embarrassed when normal adolescent boys thoughtlessly kidded him about it. Even when there is only one trainable class, it may be necessary to subdivide the class according to developmental stages and recognize these differences in the activities and printed materials used.

To secure homogeneous class organization, grading should be done on the basis of developmental levels. The most basic division is made between the "trainable" and "educable" retardates, and then recognition is given to the differences in the developmental level as measured by chronological age. With respect to the "trainable" class, some criteria regarding eligibility for enrolment is necessary, since some retarded children cannot even function in a special class. The criteria suggested by Johnson and Capiobianco[4] regarding eligibility for admission to classes for "trainable" children in the public schools is a helpful guide for the churches.

Each child should be ambulatory and toilet-trained, be able to communicate his wants, understand class instructions, and "participate in group activities without harming either himself or others within the group." Furthermore, children with personality problems indicative of emotional disturbance rather than severe mental retardation are to be excluded. Though functioning on a retarded level, an emotionally disturbed child presents special problems that most Sunday school teachers are unprepared to handle.

Grading according to developmental levels is absolutely necessary. Though maturation may be somewhat slower than normal, educable retardates do pass through discernible developmental stages, such as preadolescence, adolescence, and adulthood. With respect to separate classes for these, the general feeling of Christian educators is that they can be integrated into regular classes if they are given special attention and allowances are made for their slowness. However, this view is open to considerable question. Their limited mental development, which most often becomes apparent at school age, clearly separates them from children with average development. A normal nine-year-old reads on a third- or fourth-grade level, while an "educable" nine-year-old reads on a first-grade level, if at all. Hopefully they can be integrated, but this should not be taken as a general principle to be followed in every situation.

The structure given to a particular class should be appropriate to the educational and developmental level and should involve the whole person—mentally, physically, socially, and spiritually. In obvious disregard of these principles, one teacher boasted of holding an "opening assembly" for the trainable retardates in her Sunday school class. She seemed also to equate the success of the special class with the number of Bible verses learned by the students.

The purpose of the class structure is to lead the pupils in achieving definite goals within their capabilities, thus giving them a sense of accomplishment and providing a foundation for future achievements. Also, a structured class gives the students a sense of security because they know what to expect.

In classes for the trainable the emphasis is on social experience and adjustment. They cannot be expected to master much knowledge of the Bible or theology. Almost all of these persons are brain-damaged, are usually hyperactive, distractible, and have a short attention span. A dependable routine should be established which includes several brief activities. Some schedules suggested have included group games, a story time, activity, refreshment time, rest period, music time, and free play. A more flexible schedule may be used with older, high-level trainable retardates.

The approach used with educable retarded children is similar to that used with normal children except that the activities and materials must be geared to the mental age rather than the chronological age. For example, with a group of twelve-year-olds, activities appropriate for first- or second-year Primaries would be used instead of Junior material. With adolescents, the difficulty of the material will not exceed that used for late Primaries or Juniors. Class activities though should recognize their advanced social interest and include the planning and execution of projects such as socials, plays, singing for another class, and making gifts or preparing a basket for shut-ins.

Methods and techniques, as well as class organization and structure, should be appropriate to the educational and developmental level of the students. This is the foundation of meaningful Christian education for the retarded. Almost every teaching method or technique normally used in Christian education can be used with the mentally retarded, provided it is appropriate for the mental age. For example, with retarded children who do not read, activities and methods would be those used with preschool children. With those who read and write, activities requiring academic skills, such as reading the Bible or making notebooks and posters, could be used effectively.

Usage of the Bible and Christian doctrine are also determined by the educational and developmental level. For example, the story of Zacchaeus would be taught with a different emphasis to children, adolescents, and adults. With children, the emphasis would be on the friendliness of Jesus. With adolescents, the emphasis might be on honesty. With older adolescents and adults, the deeper implications of sin, guilt, and forgiveness could be explored.

The dynamic and interpersonal qualities of the biblical stories and Christian doctrine should be related to the actual life situations of the retarded rather than being taught as abstract truths. The story of Jesus in the Temple is an excellent illustration of relationship to authority. The parable of the talents demonstrates the meaning of trustworthiness. What does it mean for retarded persons to be trustworthy? With small children it may mean nothing more than minding their parents or picking up their toys, but with older children and adolescents it may mean doing their schoolwork well, reporting to work on time, or carrying out their assignments in Sunday school. The lessons on authority and trustworthiness are related in that the more trustworthy and responsible one is the more independently he can function. If the discussion has been guided effectively, the teacher has helped the students to accept limitations, acknowledge legitimate authority, and strive for privileges on the basis of their ability to handle them.

An effective Christian education program for mentally retarded persons in the local church is governed by the same principles operative in the total educational ministry of the church. This special ministry is an integral part of the church's program. When possible, retarded persons are integrated into regular classes, but separate classes, when necessary, are organized and structured according to the developmental and educational level of the students.

The Qualifications and Training of Teachers

The successful implementation of any Christian education program ultimately depends upon the teacher. This is particularly true in mental retardation where almost no printed teacher helps are available. The teacher is thrust back on his own resources and creative ability. It is imperative, therefore, that churches carefully screen and train persons selected to teach the retarded.

Qualifications.—In selecting teachers to staff special classes, churches are tempted to adopt extreme policies. At one extreme is the belief that only professionally trained and qualified persons should teach the retarded. One minister who believed that the church should provide religious training for the retarded qualified his answer by saying: "Special training would be required, of course." At the other extreme is the belief that the most basic qualification is the teacher's sense of "calling." One pastor feels that a religious ministry to the retarded could be undertaken only "by someone who has a special burden and qualification for such."

Both of these extreme views are to be avoided. Neither special training nor a special call is sufficient qualification in itself. Most churches will be dependent upon lay persons to staff special classes and should not hesitate to use such persons. Institutional chaplains and many churches are presently making extensive use of untrained lay persons as religious teachers. However, churches should carefully screen the teachers on the basis of competence, emotional maturity, and religious faith.

Churches first should require teachers who work with the retarded to meet the same qualifications as all other Sunday school teachers. Teaching retarded persons is as demanding, and often more so, than teaching normal persons. Persons unqualified to work in other departments of the Sunday school should not be utilized in the special department. Pastors have recognized the need for qualified workers. A suburban pastor described his participation in the creation of a special program. "I tried to be helpful in arranging for a very choice room in which the class met and was quite willing to give up good workers from other areas of the church life for this project." In another instance, a large urban church utilized professional persons within the congregation. The superintendent of the special department was a social worker; other workers included a medical doctor and registered nurse.

In the absence of qualified church workers or professional persons, the church may be tempted to utilize parents of retarded children. However, it seems unwise to allow parents to teach their own or other retarded children unless absolutely necessary. Parents often tend to be overly involved with their children and will unrealistically evaluate the child's potential or handicap. Furthermore, parents need to be freed from the care of this child so that they may participate in the life of the church.

Emotional maturity is a second qualification. Teachers must be mature enough emotionally to honestly acknowledge feelings toward retarded persons and motivations for working with them. Unless both positive and negative feelings are recognized, genuine acceptance is not likely to occur. An effective and dedicated Sunday school teacher related in a conference her difficulty in accepting one member of an educable adolescent class. The girl had a severe speech problem, was quite immature, and obviously more limited than the other class members. On several occasions the teacher considered dropping her from the class. She did not, however, because the girl seemed content and was accepted by the others. The teacher's real feelings though emerged when the special class was invited to sing before an Adult department. Afraid that the girl would act inappropriately and embarrass her, the teacher was thrown into a panic. She silently prayed that the girl would be absent, but the girl came and to the teacher's surprise was most well behaved. The teacher confessed that the real problem was her own feelings, not the girl's behavior. Actually, the teacher had never really accepted the limitations of retarded persons. But to her credit, she ackowledged these feelings and later involved the girl as an important member of her class.

In determining the emotional maturity of prospective teachers, two questions should be asked. First, does the teacher relate to the retarded as persons or as symbols? As symbols, the retarded are viewed as "special" persons. This perspective denies their basic humanity and involves the teacher in an unhealthy and unrealistic relationship. In accepting the retarded as persons, however, the teacher exercises both love and discipline, according to needs, and sets both limits and goals according to capabilities. Second, what is the teacher's motivation for working with retarded persons? Some persons teach because of pity, a sense of duty, a desire to do good, or to help the unfortunate. These are unworthy motives and should be exposed for what they are. Only persons motivated by genuine compassion and positive feeling for the retarded are to be entrusted with this responsibility.

A third qualification is a mature religious faith. Teachers must be secure in their own Christian experience and beliefs. Teaching the retarded requires a broad understanding of religious experience. The teacher must be sensitive enough to recognize the various manifestations of religious need and flexible enough to relate the gospel to these needs. When the teacher is anxious and unsure, she may respond to religious questions with stereotyped answers. For instance, a college student teaching a class of adolescent and young adult retardates interpreted a young man's question about Jesus and the church as an evangelistic opportunity. She encouraged him to respond to the invitation at the close of the church service, which he did. Later she was embarrassed when it became obvious that the young man did not understand what it meant to be a Christian or a church member. In failing to take time to explore and clarify what these concerns meant, the teacher immediately assumed that the young man needed to make a public profession of faith. She thereby ignored the need for patient and careful instruction regarding the Christian life.

Contrast, however, the way another teacher dealt with a retarded adolescent boy who was upset because his brother and a friend had torn up his radio. The boy resolved not to strike back physically, but he felt that he needed to set some limits. He also strongly believed that it was right to share your possessions and he stated that the Bible taught this. The teacher was tempted at first to fully endorse the boy's belief that he should continue to share his property as the ideal Christian response, but the teacher also knew that it was not necessarily Christian to share possessions with irresponsible persons. So the teacher supported the boy's desire to stand firm and resist exploitation.

Effective teachers of mentally retarded persons, therefore, possess three qualities: they are competent, thoroughly grounded in general Christian education principles and methods; they form consistent and warm interpersonal relationships which recognize limitations and possibilities; they are knowledgeable about the meaning of religious experience and are able to relate the gospel to specific religious concerns.

Training.—In addition to carefully screening teachers, the church is also responsible for training them to work with the mentally retarded. Inexperienced teachers should not be expected to begin a full program without orientation. As the very minimum, a training program should include consultaton with professionally trained persons, supervised contact with the retarded, and the reading of basic books on the education of the retarded.

So that the teachers can secure accurate knowledge about mental retardation and overcome personal fears, anxieties, and misconceptions, special training conferences should be organized. Ideal resource persons to lead such conferences are community professional persons. These include public schoolteachers, psychologists, social workers, physicians, and nurses. An agenda may be organized around the following topics: the nature of mental retardation, the educational and developmental levels which the retarded attain, special problems in learning, methods of teaching, management of possible nursing problems such as seizures and the special needs of parents.

For supervised contact with or observation of the mentally retarded, visits may be arranged to a special class in a neighboring church, in the public schools, or a day care center. In training volunteers to teach institutionalized retardates, this writer found that teachers were much more comfortable and secure in their role after observing a class or informally talking with retarded persons. They could then identify the retarded as persons, not as a diagnostic category.

A careful reading of the literature on the education of the retarded is also important. An excellent survey of the latest research, theories, and methods of teaching the trainable and educable is contained in *Exceptional Children in the Schools.*[5] An older but still useful book is *Educating the Retarded Child.*[6] Other books have concentrated on only one of the educational levels. Among these is *Education of the Slow-Learning Child.*[7] This book discusses the various areas of the development of the educable retardate, the philosophy and principles of education, and an educational program based on the unit method of teaching. For workers with trainable retardates, *Understanding and Teaching the Dependent Retarded Child* by Louis E. Rosenzweig and Julia Long helpfully discusses the goals of education for the retarded and outlines the minimum and maximum specific goals that can be attained with children at this level of development.

In maintaining high standards, careful screening, and adequate training, the church provides competent and committed teachers for this new ministry. It further acknowledges that the ministry to the retarded is a significant part of the church's program.

An acceptable Christian education program for the mentally retarded can only grow out of a sound philosophy. It has been maintained that one philosophy of Christian education applies to both the retarded and the normal. Religious training of the retarded must be appropriate to the level of religious development and relevant to religious needs and concerns. Churches must take their responsibility seriously enough to secure competent persons as teachers and to adequately train them. Ultimately, however, the Christian education of the retarded depends upon the motivation of the churches and their willingness to be involved in the face-to-face relationships with retarded persons. This motivation or willingness cannot be supplied through a discussion of philosophies and principles. It arises through the depths of one's commitment to Jesus Christ and involvement in his ministry.

Notes

1. Summary, State School Chaplains' Conference, Newark State School, Newark, N.Y., February 23, to March 6, 1959, memo paper, pp. 5-6.
2. Randolph Crump Miller, *Christian Nurture and the Church* (New York: Charles Scribner's Sons, 1961), p. 1.
3. Sigurd D. Petersen, *Retarded Children: God's Children* (Philadelphia: The Westminster Press, 1960), pp. 104-5.
4. Cited in Louis E. Rosenzweig and Julia Long, *Understanding and Teaching the Dependent Retarded Child* (Darien, Conn.: The Educational Publishing Corporation, 1960), p. 22.
5. Lloyd M. Dunn (ed.), *Exceptional Children in the Schools* (New York: Holt, Rinehart & Winston, 1963.)
6. Kirk and Johnson, *Educating the Retarded Child* (New York: Houghton Mifflin Co., 1951).
7. Christine P. Ingram, *Education of the Slow-Learning Child* (New York: The Ronald Press Co., 1960.)

6

Pastoral Care
of the Retarded

A comprehensive ministry to the mentally retarded incorporates both an organized Christian education program and a pastoral care ministry. Group participation and structured religious instruction as given in Christian education is only one need. An overemphasis on this facet of the church's responsibility, however, has tended to obscure the need for pastoral care. The shepherding ministry of the pastor and lay members through personal relationships with the retarded is as equally important. As with the chapter on the care of parents, the focus of the present chapter is on pastoral *care* rather than counseling. Shepherding the retarded involves several levels of ministry other than structured counseling relationships, though this is one aspect.

Pastoral Perspective Toward Retarded Persons

A realistic pastoral perspective is imperative for a full ministry to the total religious needs of the mentally retarded. The absence of a well defined shepherding ministry seems to stem from a narrow view of the church's ministry and a misunderstanding of the needs of mentally retarded persons.

Ministers sometimes fail to accept responsibility for forming pastoral relationships with the retarded persons in their congregation. In an effort to determine the extent of pastoral services given to retarded persons enrolled in special Christian classes, this writer corresponded with twenty-six pastors of churches with such classes. These were representative urban churches affiliated with the Southern Baptist Convention. With few exceptions, these ministers seemed unaware of the need of the retarded for pastoral care. In

94

some cases they seemed to have had little or no contact with the special class at all. Rather, the church's ministry consisted entirely of the organized educational program, often left in the hands of lay members or the minister of education.

Ministers, however, cannot absolve themselves of responsibility for pastoral care simply because the church sponsors special Christian education classes. Mentally retarded persons are entitled to the full ministry of the church, including pastoral attention at times of sickness and bereavement, and pastoral guidance regarding personal, vocational, and religious problems. As one minister rightly recognized, "being mentally retarded does not discount the fact that they are human and need spiritual guidance." And such guidance is the pastor's responsibility.

Pastoral responsibility is also often denied because the pastoral needs of the retarded are misunderstood. In the survey of 220 clergymen, previously mentioned, two qualifications were frequently made reflecting reservation about the extent to which a pastor either could or should be involved with mentally retarded persons.

One qualification was that a pastoral ministry to the retarded is limited by the degree to which the person is retarded. This is a valid criterion. However, the underlying assumption of some ministers seems to be that the mentally retarded always remain children, maintaining children's interests and needs. One minister commented that pastoral care "must be on a surface level . . . similar to the pastoral relation with preschool or Primary age (grade 1-3) children."

Pastoral relationships, however, are governed not only by the degree of retardation or educational level but also by the developmental level and life situation. With the retarded, as with the normal members of the congregation, the pastor's role varies according to the chronological age of the person and the problems encountered in his daily life and interpersonal relationships. Mentally retarded persons do not remain children but become adolescents and adults. The social and interpersonal concerns to which religion is applied and for which pastoral attention is required emerge from the life stage which the retarded have attained. The need for this broad approach will be more apparent in the section on specific pastoral care opportunities when we examine, for instance, the premarital and marital care of "educable" adults.

The second qualification was that a minister should have special training before effecting a pastoral ministry to the mentally retarded. A clergyman, for example, believed that such a ministry was possible "when and if the pastor is qualified," while another minister suggested that "most ministers do not have the proper training." The unspoken assumption seemed to be that the retarded are either "sick" or so different from normal persons that special training is necessary before a helping relationship can be established. It was assumed that the traditional ministries which the pastor extends to other members of his congregation were not appropriate for the retarded unless the pastor, in a sense, became more than a pastor.

Mentally retarded persons are neither "sick" nor so different from normal persons that the pastor must have special training before effecting a pastoral relationship. My own thesis, and that of other professional workers in mental retardation, is that the retarded are simply persons at the lower range of the intelligence continuum which embraces the whole population. As genuine human beings, they can therefore be as emotionally healthy or unhealthy as other persons. Emotional forces which nurture emotional health or ill health are the same for both the retarded and normal. The measure of health is that a person reach the peak of his own powers, that the actual functions performed are consistent to his own capacities.[1] In short, the retarded are more like us than they are different from us. Granting the limitations imposed by the retarded condition, the needs and concerns requiring pastoral attention are not significantly different from what the pastor encounters in other persons.

The pastor's procedure in counseling the mentally retarded, consequently, follows accepted counseling principles with modifications in the objective to meet particular needs and disabilities.

Frederick C. Thorne[2] has suggested several basic objectives relevant to pastoral counseling. Underlying any counseling procedure is the pastor's acceptance of the retardate and the seriousness of his problems. The problems may not be important to the pastor, but they are to the retarded person. Next the retardate must be allowed to express and clarify his feelings and to gain self-confidence through experiences of success. Standards for acceptable conduct should be outlined. Teaching the retarded person how to seek help when faced with insurmountable problems is also a goal.

These objectives recognize that any solution arrived at in the counseling relationship must be related to what is "internal" in the retardate and not imposed from without. A completely nondirective stance, however, cannot be assumed. Counseling the retarded involves guiding and teaching, as well as the ventilation and clarification of feeling.

The Context of Pastoral Care

Shepherding the mentally retarded involves not only acceptance of their basic humanity but also appreciation for the "context" in which pastoral care occurs. Pastoral care cannot be divorced from a context of social relationships—the church, the family, and the community.

The basic context in which pastoral care takes place is the fellowship of the church. The personal ministry of the pastor is meaningless apart from full acceptance of the retarded by the congregation, which in a sense is an "incarnation of concern." Even for persons unable to relate meaningfully to the pastor, the church's recognition that they are important is in itself a ministry both to them and to their families. The pastor's first task in the pastoral care of the retarded is the creation of an atmosphere of acceptance within the church.

How can the church and pastor create such an atmosphere? Here is what one church with a special department of sixty-five children and fifteen workers did. The ministry to retarded persons was first accepted as the entire church's ministry, not just that of the pastor or of a few lay workers. It was further recognized that a full religious ministry entailed more than just special classes meeting on Sunday morning. Consequently, two or three times a year the pastor conducts a special worship service in which the children and their families receive recognition. The children are learning reverence, respect, and honor for God and the house of God by learning to participate in the regular worship service. They are not only taught to honor God but also to honor and respect their parents and to perform meaningful work. To accomplish this, a contest is conducted by one of the organizations designed especially for retarded children. To score points in the contest certain tasks have to be performed at home, such as washing dishes, bringing in clothes, making beds, sweeping floors, dusting furniture, mowing lawns, and raking grass and leaves.

While creative programs are being developed for retarded children and adolescents, little attention has been given to adult retardates. For instance, J. E. Crane's[3] survey disclosed that no

church of any denomination in Chattanooga, Tennessee, was ministering to the retarded adult. He further found that the educable
adult receives very little from existing Adult classes, and that the
severely retarded adult just doesn't attend church. Only one severely
retarded adult out of thirty-one attended church regularly, while
none attended Sunday school.

How can the church provide for retarded adults? One teacher
recruited a twenty-one-year-old educable retarded woman as a
"helper," whose specific responsibility was keeping the class records.
Together with the Nursery leader, the teacher prepared the church
members to let Ann work with the babies in the Nursery. Her work
was so acceptable that she later baby-sat for several of the members. While care must be taken that retarded persons are not assigned more responsibility than they can manage, nevertheless, this
teacher's sensitivity and trust allowed Ann to meaningfully participate in and contribute to the life of the church.

The church, however, does not minister in isolation from the
family in which the retarded person lives. Some of the problems
which the teacher of a special class encounters may be products
of an anxious or even unconcerned family. Susan, for instance, has
been so overindulged by her mother that she is unable to endure
even the slightest frustration. When frustrated in class Susan hits
or kicks her teacher. She loves to eat and has gained so much
weight that it is difficult for her to move around; some days she
stays in bed all day. The teacher's efforts to help the mother
acknowledge the injustice she is doing Susan have been to no avail.
In the same class with Susan is an eighteen-year-old boy with a
mental age of five. Although he tries very hard to please, the
teacher feels that Sammy could learn much more if his parents
would work with him at home, which, however, they refuse to do.
As a consequence of the parents' lack of co-operation, the teacher's
work is stymied. Both of these families need sensitive pastoral care.
In Susan's situation, the family needs to maintain more realistic
discipline. In Sammy's case, the parents need to be reminded of
their obligation to help their son, even though retarded, to achieve
his maximum potential. What the church can do for these children
is limited unless the families become more responsible.

The church's acceptance of a retarded person may be the means
by which the family more genuinely accepts the child or comes to
appreciate the child's potential. One pastor reports that a retarded

child was kept in a back room, and especially when visitors were present. As a result of the interest expressed by the church, the child was not only made a part of the Sunday school, but was also brought from the back room and made a part of the family and home. Because the church accepted this child, the family realized that their loved one, though not normal, could have a part in the family life. The same pastor reports that some parents have been greatly surprised by what the children have learned. One couple who thought that their child could not memorize anything were amazed when one morning he stood and quoted the twenty-third Psalm. Another family was quite proud of their son who learned, in Sunday school, to tie his shoe for the first time.

As a significant side effect of this ministry, parents are often drawn closer to the church. In one situation, the father of two sons, members of the Exceptional Department, was rather timid and slow to become warm toward the church until the pastor and lay members began visiting in his home. He now renders some help on outings and other activities in the Exceptional Department and attends church more regularly. In another case, ministering to a retarded child helped the parents overcome religious differences. Members of different denominations, the mother united with the church providing a special class for their child, and the father is seriously considering joining. While the church must resist any temptation to exploit the needs of parents of retarded children, the ministry to the children is a visible manifestation of God's love and of the reality of Christian fellowship.

A third context in which pastoral care must be set is the community. As Golden noted: "The counseling relationship should always be seen within the context of other relationships and forces which impinge upon the retardate's life."[4] Whenever serious adjustment or emotional problems require long-term counseling or other treatment procedures, the pastor should correlate his work with other professional workers involved with the retardate. These normally would include one or more of the following: physicians, psychologists, social workers, vocational rehabilitation counselors, and special education teachers. The minister does not work with the retarded and their families apart from professional and community resources.

The basic context in which the pastoral care of the mentally retarded occurs is the church. Without genuine acceptance and compassion by the whole church, the personal ministries of the pastor and teachers are ineffective. Yet the "world" of the retarded consists of families and communities, and these factors condition the nature and extent of pastoral services. What the pastor does, therefore, is influenced by the attitude of the church, the adequacy of the family, and the resources of the community.

Specific Pastoral Care Opportunities

What specific pastoral ministries can be offered to mentally retarded persons? According to a survey of clergymen, the most frequent ministry was pastoral conversations, and this category was checked by 63 per cent of the respondents. More specific ministries were performed, however. A majority had made pastoral visits at times of sickness; 35 per cent had counseled about personal problems; and 25 per cent had counseled about vocational problems. From the pastor's perspective, the most frequent pastoral care opportunities revolve around typical crisis situations: illness and bereavement, religious decision, vocational choice, premarital and marital behavior. Additional cases illustrating the pastoral care of retardates from an institutional chaplain's perspective but relevant to the work of the community pastor are presented in chapter 7.

Illness and bereavement.—Pastoral attention in the crisis of illness or bereavement ranges from friendly visits to helping the person "work through" his grief. The most significant factor though is that the pastor care enough to express his interest. What the visit means, however, will vary according to the mental and chronological age of the person. With retarded children, the pastor may be regarded as a friendly man. This was Dr. Brown's experience with Johnny and Sally, who were in the hospital for tests.

DR. BROWN: I am looking for a little boy named Johnny and a little girl named Sally. Are you Johnny? (*Johnny moved from the window to the center of the room.*)

JOHNNY: I Johnny. (*Speech was broken and mumbled.*)

DR. BROWN: Hi, Johnny. I'm glad to meet you. I am Brother Brown, a minister or preacher. I heard that you were in the hospital and I wanted to come by and meet you so we could become friends.

JOHNNY: (*Johnny nodded.*)

DR. BROWN: Are you Sally?

SALLY: (*Nodded and made a sound.*)

DR. BROWN: Do you go to church or Sunday school?

JOHNNY: No, I don't go to Sunday school. Mommie does.

DR. BROWN: Do you like to look at the pretty book? *(Sally continued turning pages, occasionally looking my way.)* What kind of book do you have, Sally? *(By this time I realized Sally could not talk.)*
JOHNNY: Coloring book.
DR. BROWN: Where did Sally get her book?
JOHNNY: From the lady. *(Johnny pointed out the door toward a volunteer worker.)*

With adult retardates, the pastor often encounters a deeper level of concern. A minister visited a retarded man in the hospital for an operation. Since Albert's family could not be with him, the minister came two hours before the operation and remained until Albert was sedated and taken to the operating room. Although the nurse in charge reported that Albert was somewhat apprehensive, he greeted the minister warmly and told about the new friends he had made in the hospital. When asked how he felt about the operation, he replied that it would be all right. The operating doctor had been to see him and explained the procedure. It would be good though if he had someone to pray for him. The minister stated that he could certainly perform this service. They both bowed their heads and the minister prayed for God's guidance upon the doctors and nurses and for his watchcare over Albert. After the operation, when Albert saw his brother, the pastor's visit and prayer comprised the first part of the conversation.

The crisis of bereavement presents more serious problems. In this crisis, the pastor can be of significant assistance to both the retarded and the family. The bereavement response of the mentally retarded is similar to the bereavement of normal persons. Their family relationships are quite meaningful, and the death of a family member is a traumatic experience which must be treated with honesty and sensitivity. While death will be of little significance to severely retarded persons unable to form personal relationships, older, higher-level retardates must be told of the death, guided through the funeral, and supported during the postfuneral adjustment. Effective pastoral care respects the feelings of the retarded person and his right to be informed.

The sister of a retarded woman, for instance, recognized the advisability of careful preparation before the death of their mother, who was incurably ill. She periodically informed the retarded sister of the worsening condition of the mother and immediately notified her of the death. Since it was felt that attendance at the funeral might be too much of a strain, the sister was taken to the funeral home before the funeral to see the body of her mother. A few days later she went to the cemetery. Although the pain of bereavement could not be avoided, the sister's thoughtfulness contributed to the ease with which the retarded sister worked through her grief.

A distinct service which the pastor can perform is to allow the retarded person to ventilate his feelings. Although the father of a retarded woman had been in ill health for some time, his death came unexpectedly. His daughter harbored strong resentment against him because she felt that he had been "partial" to the other children. The minister was chosen to break the news. After breaking the news of the death gently, he led her to talk about these hostile feelings. The minister listened but neither justified the father's actions nor the daughter's resentment. He reminded her, however, that this was a difficult time for her mother, and that she, too, needed support. The daughter acknowledged that was true and promised to be considerate and understanding, which she did.

The pastoral care of the mentally retarded in the crisis of illness or bereavement is a ministry of support and comfort. Such a ministry recognizes the retarded's need for meaningful relationships in trying situations and is extended to all persons regardless of the mental or chronological age. The only limitation is the retarded's degree of responsiveness to personal attention. However, in the following discussion of the remaining three pastoral care opportunities, it will be apparent that in these situations the pastor's ministry is guided by the retardate's degree of responsibility, social maturity, and intellectual capacity.

Religious decision.—The ministry to the retarded at the point of religious decision requires judgment regarding the degree of religious responsibility. What do ministers believe about the religious responsibility of the mentally retarded? Ninety per cent of the clergymen surveyed believed that the retarded are capable of understanding what it means to be a Christian and of becoming a member of the church. Of the total number of ministers, 43 per cent had already received retarded persons as members of their churches. An additional 49 per cent indicated that they would be willing to do so in the future. In general, it was believed that the retardation should not be a basis for excluding a person from church membership. The decision for accepting or rejecting these persons should be made on their ability to understand what they are doing.

Questions of religious responsibility arise at the point of determining eligibility for confirmation or believer's baptism. Current Protestant practices must be considered from the viewpoint of churches which practice infant baptism and confirmation and those which practice believer's baptism. The Lutheran Church will be taken as representative of churches practicing infant baptism and confirmation and the Baptists as representative of those practicing believer's baptism.

In Lutheran practice, as we have seen, only persons ready to be communicant members are confirmed, and the same requirements made of normal persons were applied to the retarded. The consensus seemed to be that only educable adult retardates were capable of receiving the Lord's Supper. It was suggested that a retardate should not be enrolled in a confirmation class prior to sixteen years of age. Thus the principal pastoral responsibility consists of determining when the retarded is ready to be included in the confirmation class, of instructing the class or securing another teacher, and of approving the retarded for confirmation. Confirmation classes provide a structured procedure for judging the readiness of a person to be a communicant.

In the free church tradition which practices believer's baptism and encourages "spontaneous" decisions more informal and unstructured methods are used. In this tradition, the basic problem is that of initiative. Does the church, through the pastor and teachers, move toward the retarded in encouraging a "profession of faith" or does the church wait for the retarded person to indicate a personal interest. Both procedures are followed. The institutionalized retardates attending a community church, described in chapter 4, took the initiative in requesting church membership. The concern and interest arose in the individuals and the church responded to their movements. In another situation, the church moved toward the retarded. The retarded persons, members of a special Sunday school department, had received careful religious instruction and had been accepted by other church members. During a series of revival services, the educable adolescents whom the teacher felt were capable and ready to make a public profession of faith in Christ were encouraged to do so. During the course of several months, many of the members of the special class joined the church. In both situations, careful attention was given to the readiness and ability of these retardates to make a responsible religious decision. Moreover, reception into church membership was preceded by religious instruction.

Churches practicing believer's baptism may, however, fall into one of two pitfalls. First, an emphasis on conversion, on having an emotional experience, may stir up feelings of guilt and anxiety which the retarded are not emotionally or mentally equipped to handle. Second, the church may assume that the verbalization of the right words, i.e., "I am saved" or "I trust in Jesus" is tantamount to an understanding of their meaning. The need for careful interpretation and teaching regarding the meaning of the Christian life is ignored.

Baptism and reception into church membership should be preceded by inclusion in a Christian education class for an appropriate period of time and by pastoral conversations. A few questions asked hurriedly at the front of the church during the invitation is inadequate pastoral guidance. In at least one private conversation the pastor should explore the retardate's understanding of the Christian life and church membership, the motivation for becoming a church member, and the relevance of this decision to his personal and social life. Through careful pastoral attention, baptism and church membership become meaningful experiences, not a "magical rite" or the "thing to do." Without such attention, the church is guilty of irresponsible evangelism.

Consider, for example, these two retarded persons.

When a twenty-five-year-old retarded woman approached a minister about becoming a member of the church, he expressed delight that she was interested. He learned that this had been on her mind for several months. When she was younger, she had a quick temper and often "cussed" when she got mad. She now knew that this was wrong. She loved the Lord and wanted to live right. The minister interpreted that it was only through God's love for us and through our faith in Jesus that we could live pleasing to him. She replied that she already knew this, and this was why she wanted to be baptized. Although she did not use the "right words," the minister felt that she did understand in her own way the meaning of being a Christian. Acceptance into the fellowship of the church supported her resolve to put aside childish behavior and become a responsible adult.

In contrast, when an educable retardate in late adolescence was asked why she wanted to be baptized, she shook her head and said that she didn't know. The pastor replied that she could not be baptized until she was clear about its meaning and why it was important to her. It would be good if she would mention this concern to the Sunday school teacher. Then the entire class could study the meaning of baptism and church membership. After this the pastor would be happy to discuss the matter with her again.

The pastoral care of the mentally retarded at this point of religious decision requires a balance of patience and responsibility. Though responsible for carefully teaching the nature of the Christian faith, the church must wait patiently for the movement of God's Spirit to issue in personal religious concern. In maintaining the usual church procedure for receiving members, allowances must be made for the retarded's intellectual limited ability. This conditions how "saving faith" is understood and expressed.

Vocational habilitation.—Pastoral concern for the mentally retarded encompasses every aspect of the retardate's life with religious dimensions. Most important of these include the retarded's vocational choice and his relationship with the opposite sex. Work as a "God-appointed function of human life" is one medium through which retarded persons become useful and constructive citizens. In helping the retarded become socially responsible through gainful employment, the pastor occupies a unique function. First of all, he is durably related to the family and knows the total family situation, which may be either a help or a hindrance to the retardate seeking to function more independently.

Second, the pastor as a teacher can relate the Christian doctrine of vocation to the specific needs of the retarded. To the "professional" family who feels that janitorial work is beneath the dignity of their retarded son, the pastor may need to interpret the Protestant view that all work is honorable which serves the good of men. For the family who overprotects and shields their child from assuming appropriate responsibility, the pastor may need to remind them that every person has a right to find fulfilment in meaningful work.

Whatever vocational guidance the pastor performs, however, should be in co-operation with appropriate professional workers and community agencies. The vocational habilitation of the mentally retarded is a long-term, delicate process which must be carefully handled. Thus, the pastor may find that his ministry does more harm than good if he attempts to be totally responsible for the habilitation procedure. For instance, a minister assumed that vocational guidance was simply a matter of getting a person a job. He allowed an educable retarded eighteen-year-old cerebral palsied girl to take her specially built typewriter to the church twice a week for typing a list of names for use in church programs. Although the girl was the client of a vocational rehabilitation counselor, the minister neglected to consult with him. Consequently, the minister was unaware of the extent of the retardation and of the girl's inability to accept her physical limitations. The typing job became quite boring. When the counselor offered to help, the relationship was terminated. Severe personality problems began to develop, and the minister was called night and day by the family to help calm the girl. He could not understand why she didn't respond as he expected. Then he discovered that although she was eighteen chronologically, she was not that old intellectually. As this minister discovered, vocational habilitation is more than just securing a job. It involves the total personality, including emotional stability, mental ability, and physical health.

The first task of the pastor, therefore, is referral to appropriate professional workers or community agencies. Of these the most important are special education departments in the public schools, the Office of Vocational Rehabilitation, and the local association for retarded children. In making referrals and mobilizing the family to take some action, the pastor must be careful not to assume complete responsibility. One pastor, for instance, was manipulated by a family into providing transportation service. He took the retarded man to the vocational rehabilitation counselor's office for all the interviews and to the doctor's office for the medical examination. In the counselor's judgment the family had taken advantage of the pastor's desire to be of assistance. The counselor recognized that mental retardates and their families sometimes need assistance when in a "tight spot"; however, they must invest something of themselves in getting the client to appointments through their own means. If the client and/or his family are not willing to do this, there are few chances of successfully rehabilitating the client. Ministers should be careful to analyze the families who continually request them to transport them from place to place and guard against being used by individuals who are willing to take all they can without putting forth any effort whatever.

More realistic limits were set by another minister on the services he felt responsible for performing. The pastor referred a thirty-year-old educable mentally retarded man to the Division of Vocational Rehabilitation. The client was a janitor in the rural church of the pastor. The pastor accompanied the client to the counselors' office for the initial interview and was responsible for his getting to the doctor's office for the routine medical examination, since the family was physically unable to do this. Then the pastor dropped out completely as the counselor worked directly with the client and his family. Successfully rehabilitated, the retardate is presently employed, earning about thirty dollars per week.

At least three benefits result from referral to professional workers with the retarded. First of all, a thorough evaluation is made of the retardate's ability, including physical, educational, and psychological. It is important to determine the degree of mental retardation, along with physical handicaps. In some cases physical handicaps thought to be permanent have been corrected through surgery. In others the correction of a hearing or visual handicap has enabled the retarded person to function more adequately. Second, the counselor can arrange for appropriate job training through special education departments, sheltered workshops, or trade schools. Finally, the retardate can then be placed in a job appropriate to his abilities, and supervised during the initial adjustment period.

The second task of the pastor is follow-up. Both the family and the retardate need support, encouragement, and guidance long after the training program is begun. Parents often have doubts about the ability of their child to function semi-independently or independently. On the other hand, they may expect the training agency to perform a miracle with their child. Between these two extremes, the pastor encourages them to realistically appraise the ability of the child and to permit him to exercise freedom appropriate to his degree of responsibility.

The pastor should not forget that the retarded person is often fearful and conditioned to failure. He needs encouragement to be his "best self." When he fails, the pastor can help him recognize where he contributed to the failure and where he was failed by other persons involved. For instance, a retarded woman accepted a job in a nursing home, caring for elderly persons. Although she was quite capable, personal conflict with the supervisor resulted in her dismissal. In conversation with her pastor, she acknowledged that she was partly responsible because of her quick temper. She also knew that the supervisor was impatient and abusive with her.

The minister supported the reality of her judgment and actions. She should not tolerate abusive behavior, but, on the other hand, she was wrong in provoking such behavior.

The pastor's work in the vocational habilitation of the retarded is grounded on the biblical view that work is honorable and a means of personal fulfilment. Recognizing that genuine rehabilitation involves the functional wholeness of the total personality and not simply the ability to perform a job, the pastor utilizes the services of professional and community resources. He may initiate the relationship or serve as a liaison until the family is able to assume responsibility. Whatever the role, continual pastoral support is given to the family's efforts to educate and train their child.

Sex education, premarital guidance, and marital counseling.— Ministering at the time of religious decision and vocational habilitation presupposes that retarded persons can assume some degree of personal responsibility for their actions. Religious decision implies responsibility before God, while vocational habilitation presupposes social responsibility. The mentally retarded are not only related to God, the church, and the community but are also related to other persons as sexual beings. What are the pastoral care implications of the sexual development and identity of the mentally retarded?

A realistic appreciation for the sexual needs of the retarded has been prevented by the prevalence of two stereotypes. The first is the belief that mentally retarded persons are "eternal" children. Their developmental growth into adolescence and adulthood with accompanying sexual maturity is ignored. A second stereotype reflects the opposite view. Adolescent and adult retardates are regarded as "animals" with uncontrollable sexual passion. Institutionalizing retardates, particularly females in prime childbearing age, is sometimes justified on the basis of this mistaken view. It is true that some retarded persons do not develop sexual interests while others are sexually promiscuous, but categorical judgments about *all* mentally retarded persons are to be avoided. Sexual maturity is relative to the educational and developmental level. Responsibility for sexual behavior is achieved in the same manner as responsibility for personal and social behavior. Thus the principles of sex education, premarital guidance, and marital counseling of the retarded do not differ appreciably from accepted practices for normal persons.

The church is responsible for teaching mentally retarded persons the religious significance of their sexual identity and the Christian understanding of responsible sexual behavior. This should not usually be done as a separate course on sex education. Rather, it can be incorporated into regular curriculum material or discussed in pastoral conversations about the retardate's life goals. In the course of a year at least one lesson in the Christian education program should deal with "Who am I?"

Retardates need to know that they have physical desires, spiritual strivings, and emotional needs. They need to be told that all of the feelings which we have are good because this is the way that God made us. God, however, expects us to be responsible for our actions. As there are appropriate ways to express our anger, so God has ordained appropriate ways to express our sexual needs. To be in the "image of God," as Karl Barth contends, is to be created a man or a woman. It is to have a sexual identity. For younger and more severely retarded persons it will be enough that they identify themselves as a boy or girl. Adolescent and adult high-level trainable and educable retardates often need more explicit instruction.

What is taught regarding responsible sexual behavior will be influenced by the person's interest as manifested by his questions and behavior and by his mental ability and chronological age. When overt sexual misconduct is demonstrated, the pastor will deal with this problem directly and forthrightly. For instance, a minister was asked to talk with two educable retarded adolescents who had been caught in the act of sexual intercourse. In talking with each separately, he accepted the legitimacy of their sexual needs, but placed their action in a broader context than their desire for one another. Although sex is good because God made us that way, sexual relationships are reserved for marriage. One result of their action might be the birth of a child, and they are not capable at this time of caring for a child. Their act, therefore, is unacceptable because they cannot assume responsibility for its consequences.

A more difficult problem is posed when adult retardates decide to marry. What does the pastor do when he is asked to perform a marriage ceremony for a mentally retarded couple? Should he perform the ceremony if they have obtained a marriage license and have the legal right? Should he categorically refuse?

At this point it will be helpful to review some of the research regarding marriage and parenthood of the mentally retarded. Available research data on this topic was recently investigated and reported by Medora Steedman Bass.[5] The consensus of opinion was "that marriage can be recommended for retarded individuals in an appreciable per cent of cases, but that it is often advisable to prevent parenthood."

On the basis of this data, the minister must evaluate each retarded couple on the merits of their motivation and ability to maintain a home. For the minister's own protection and for the welfare of the couple, two steps should be taken at the very outset. First of all, the legality of a marriage between two mentally retarded persons must be clarified. The Bass study showed that "marriage for the 'weak-minded' is prohibited in Iowa, Pennsylvania, and South Dakota; and is probably illegal in fifteen other states." Second, the minister should share the responsibility for this decision with leaders of the church and other professional persons. Community agencies and professional workers with whom the retardates have had previous contact are helpful resources. Consultations may be arranged with other persons, such as a psychologist, social welfare worker, physician, and vocational rehabilitation counselor.

The first question the minister should ask is in regard to the couple's ability to maintain a home and themselves at a reasonable standard of living. To satisfactorily answer this question, it is necessary to determine their personal maturity and social responsibility. If the minister is satisfied that the couple can be successfully married, the next problem is to determine whether pregnancy is contraindicated. While many retardates are capable of being adequate marriage partners, they are not always capable of being parents. Bass says that "the psychological stress of the responsibilities of parenthood, especially with many children, may disrupt the precarious adjustment of the retardate."[6] Decisions regarding birth control methods, whether mechanical or surgical, must be made by a physician. Legal, medical, and moral considerations of sterilization, when this procedure is indicated, is to be dealt with in relation to specific couples and not on the basis of generalities.

Discussions of sterilization, sexual behavior, and management of the retarded often generate strong feelings based on misinformation and prejudice. It is time, therefore, that we recognize the right of mentally retarded persons to live as normal a life as their capabilities permit. In some cases, this means that they be permitted to marry, with adequate precautions taken to prevent the birth of children when this is deemed wise.

A pastor's decision to marry a retarded couple is based on the same criteria which he employs with normal persons: Can the couple assume the responsibility of marriage? However, the pastor's premarital guidance of the couple should be carefully structured and possible problem areas thoroughly discussed. In addition to the decision regarding children, guidance is needed about the budgeting of money, the use of leisure time, the management of personal differences, and the Christian understanding of marriage as a covenant relationship under God—involving a lifetime commitment to the mutual care of each other. The pastor should also make explicit his continuing concern for the couple even after the marriage ceremony and his availability when overwhelming problems arise.

Marriage counseling procedures with the mentally retarded are similar to those employed in the marital guidance of normal persons. Sometimes though, a more direct or teaching approach is often necessary. The pastor's task includes the clarification of feelings, the localizing of specific problems, exploring possible solutions, and referral to appropriate professional workers and community agencies when long-term or intensive help is indicated. How one pastor supported a couple and their family is shown in this case study. The wife is obviously retarded while the husband appears to be in the dull normal range. This case, however, should not be taken to be representative of all marriages involving mentally retarded persons.

When Dr. Smith first met Sue and Bill, they were living with Mrs. Jones, Bill's mother. The pastor's first awareness that Sue was mentally retarded came through observation of her behavior while eating in the home of Mrs. Jones. Sue never ate dinner with the family. She just sat in the living room and watched television. She spoke only when spoken to and took no initiative in caring for her infant daughter.

Informal pastoral contacts were maintained through visits in the home and through Sue and Bill's attendance at church, of which only Sue was a member. Active pastoral participation in the couple's life came when Sue was committed to a state hospital for the mentally ill. Several events preceded this crisis. In January Sue's mother and Mrs. Jones "had it out." Sue's mother accused Mrs. Jones of mistreating Sue and of stealing money from her. Mrs. Jones told the mother never to come back. In the fall Bill built a makeshift house across the field from Mrs. Jones. They moved there in December. About this time it was also learned that Sue was pregnant again, and the baby was born in March.

What effect having total responsibility for maintaining a home and two children had on Sue's emotional disturbance can only be surmised. But in April Mrs. Jones found Sue washing windows with a brand new dress which she had bought for the oldest girl. Two weeks later the pastor discovered that Sue had been sucking the blood to the surface of the baby's face and arms. As she explained it, "I just love the baby so much I guess I just kiss it too hard." The next month Sue set fire to the field between their house and Mrs. Jones's in retaliation at Bill for spending the afternoon with his mother. At this time the pastor interpreted to Bill and Mrs. Jones that Sue was not "just mean" as they thought. She was sick and needed the attention of a doctor. In the last week of May, Sue dropped the baby, knocking her arm out of the socket and causing severe bruises around the ears and neck. The doctor to whom the baby was taken reported the incident to the county law officials. They agreed not to prosecute if Sue would be committed to the state hospital in a neighboring city.

Sue remained in the hospital only five weeks. Upon returning home, she still reacted violently to certain situations and remained apathetic toward her infant daughter, cared for now by Mrs. Jones's daughter. The pastor decided to visit in the home to learn firsthand what the present situation was, to demonstrate his continuing concern for Sue, since the community had withdrawn from her. He wanted to encourage her to continue participation in the church, and he wanted also to encourage her husband to be sympathetic and faithful in this time of illness. Prior to the visit the pastor talked with Mrs. Jones, Bill, and one of the deacons. He also wrote the chaplain at the state hospital for information and suggestions.

The pastor met with Sue and Bill in the living room of their home. It was unkempt and still unfinished, though they had been living there for almost a year. The visit lasted fifty minutes, and the pastor described it as "relaxed and very conversational." The excerpts selected from the pastor's verbatim account of the visit illustrate his attempts to deal with specific problems. After a brief period of casual conversation, the pastor asks:

PASTOR: Sue, do you feel like the doctor helped you much this summer?
SUE: Yes, I feel better.

BILL: That was a pretty place down there. Big yards and a lot of nice buildings. You wouldn't think a place like that would be pretty, but it was.

PASTOR: *(Sue is out of the room.)* Does Sue seem to be getting along better?

BILL: She does since I had it out with her mother. Her mother was the cause of Sue getting sick. Every time she came over Sue would get all up in the air and tear things up. I just told her mother not to come around too much.

PASTOR: What does Sue think of that?

BILL: She doesn't care. She never said anything. *(Sue comes back.)*

PASTOR: Sue, are you going to keep Mary soon. *(Mary is the child staying with Bill's sister.)*

SUE: Oh, I don't know. Norma and Tom are keeping her. They would hate to give her up. I don't think I could do much with her now.

PASTOR: You think Norma is taking care of her all right?

SUE: She seems happy with her. *(Sue leaves the room again.)*

PASTOR: Bill, you said Sue was upset when her mother came to visit.

BILL: Yes. Her mother is the cause of it all. She always has tried to step between us. She is that way with all her children. Sue's brother and sister both had to set her straight. She almost split up the marriage of Sue's sister. She caused them to get a divorce. They were divorced for two years, but are now back together.

PASTOR: Does she seem to try to run her children?

BILL: When she would come, she told Sue to pay no attention to me. I told Sue one thing, she told her another. Anyone would be confused. Finally, I just had it out with her. She still visits, but only for a few minutes.

PASTOR: Do you think you will bring the baby home soon?

BILL: I don't know. Sue still flares up every once in a while, and does things she shouldn't. I don't think she ought to have the baby for a while.

PASTOR: But does she seem better than before she went to the hospital?

BILL: Oh, yes.

PASTOR: Was the doctor able to help you discover the reason for Sue's behavior?

BILL: I only got to talk to him once, and he told me he couldn't find what was wrong.

In concluding the visit, the pastor assured both Sue and Bill of his continuing interest in them and lifted up their concerns before God in prayer. He made a tentative appointment to call again in about three weeks. As to future ministries, Dr. Smith decided on two courses of action. First, he would maintain social contact through periodic visits in the home. Second, he planned to consult with Sue's family doctor, and if the present behavior persisted, to suggest further psychiatric treatment.

Without minimizing the deeper dynamics which may be present, Sue's "acting out" behavior seems to have resulted from the assumption of responsibility in excess of her capacities and the conflict created by her mother. When these pressures are removed, she should be able to make a marginal adjustment.

In this situation, the pastor performed at least three distinct services. First, he had been a trusted friend, committed to the interests of all parties. Second, he "interpreted" Sue's behavior to the family so that they could act responsibly toward her. Third, he effected referrals to and co-operated with professional persons involved. In essence, the pastor was involved in the total life of his members.

What pastoral care ministries are performed reflects the church's understanding of its responsibility and the need of mentally retarded persons. Underlying this chapter is the conviction that the church is responsible for effecting a total ministry to the retarded, geared to their educational and developmental level and appreciative of their physical, emotional, and social needs. Pastoral care services are set in the context of the church, the family, and the community. Specific pastoral care opportunities include illness and bereavement, religious decision, vocational habilitation, sex education, premarital guidance, and marriage counseling. Being mentally retarded does not exclude one from the full ministry of the church. It only conditions the nature and extent of that ministry.

Notes

1. Seward Hiltner, "The New Concern of Recent Years," *The Church and Mental Health*, ed. Paul B. Maves (New York: Charles Scribner's Sons, 1953), p. 73.

2. Frederick C. Thorne, "Counseling and Psychotherapy with Mental Defectives," *Counseling and Psychotherapy with the Mentally Retarded*, ed. Chalmers L. Stacey and Manfred F. DeMartino (Glencoe, Ill.: The Free Press, 1957), pp. 77-78.

3. J. E. Crane, Chattanooga, Tennessee, personal correspondence, October 25, 1963.

4. Edward S. Golden, "Pastoral Counseling and Guidance with the Mental Retardate," *Pastoral Psychology*, September, 1962, p. 32.

5. Medora Steedman Bass, "Marriage, Parenthood, and Prevention of Pregnancy," *American Journal of Mental Deficiency*, November, 1963, pp. 318 ff.

6. *Ibid.*, p. 321.

7

Institutional
Ministry

A religious ministry to the mentally retarded extends beyond those residing in the community and served by local churches. It includes the approximately two hundred thousand retarded persons living in public and private residential institutions. Little recognition, however, has been given to the religious needs of institutionalized retardates or to the adequacy of the religious ministry which they receive. In many instances, the religious care of institutionalized retardates is delegated to community pastors and churches who have no formal relation to the hospital nor training for work with the retarded. More recently it has been recognized that such a ministry should be administered by a clergyman, employed by the hospital in a full-time capacity. This trend though is often characterized by the mistaken assumption that any minister who can be an effective pastor can also be an effective chaplain to institutionalized retardates.

Appropriate denominational agencies and state and local associations of churches should encourage residential institutions to provide competent chaplaincy services. They should actively co-operate with the chaplain and institution in developing a comprehensive religious ministry. Responsibility for the religious care of institutionalized retardates should be entrusted to a clinically trained minister, employed in a full-time capacity as the institutional chaplain. He is the key to an effective religious ministry.

Current Chaplaincy Services

The number of state institutions employing full-time chaplains has sharply increased during the past few years. In 1959, Lawson[1] surveyed forty-three state institutions which were providing full-time chaplaincy programs for their mentally retarded residents. In thirty-eight institutions he found thirty-eight Protestant, fifteen Roman Catholic, and four Jewish chaplains serving on a full-time basis. In addition, there were fifty-three part-time chaplains working in forty state schools. This marks an increase of over 200 per cent since 1954, when only seventeen full-time chaplains were employed. The responsibilities of these chaplains centered around leading worship, directing religious education programs, and performing pastoral ministries.

These figures indicate that the importance of a religious ministry to institutionalized retardates is generally recognized. Developing an adequate chaplaincy service, however, is hindered by at least three obstacles.[2] The first is the absence of a clearly defined role of who the chaplain is and what he does. The role of the Protestant chaplain is still emerging and has not yet crystallized into a definite pattern. Of the several factors contributing to this lack of clarity, one is that the chaplain's work with institutionalized retardates is relatively new. He has, in many instances, been forced to formulate his own role without much assistance from either the hospital he serves or the religious organization which he represents. A second factor is the absence of a strong professional organization to set standards and qualifications for chaplains serving institutions for the retarded. Such standards were set for general hospital chaplains by the American Protestant Hospital Association and for mental hospital chaplains by the Association of Mental Hospital Chaplains. In 1961, plans were made to organize a separate chaplain's section in the American Association on Mental Deficiency. Hopefully, this group will recommend standards for chaplains and conceptualize more adequately the chaplain's role. A third factor is the differing views of hospital administrators. They are not clear themselves as to the role of the chaplain, or they tend to interpret the chaplain's function in light of their own religious background without sufficient regard for the "context" of the institution.

The second obstacle is the absence of a clear definition of the chaplain's relation to the institution. A recent survey by Edward Golden[3] demonstrated this problem. Golden surveyed the quality of the services rendered by forty-three full-time chaplains of state institutions for the retarded and their relation to the institution which they served. He viewed the chaplain's role in terms of a continuum. At one end of the continuum the chaplain would be integrally involved in the total institutional program, and at the other end his services would be considered an ancillary service. His own personal belief was that a clinically trained chaplain should be integrally related to the institutional program rather than function in an ancillary way. Of the forty-two chaplains participating in the study, however, only nine were functioning in an integrative-co-operative team relationship; thirteen had achieved a partial integrative-co-operative relationship, and the remainder had non-collaborative relationships.

Golden found that the chaplain's relation to the hospital, the hospital's orientation toward patient care, and the administrator's expectations of the chaplain directly influenced the quality of the services rendered. Chaplains who functioned broadly or in an integrated way with the professional staff had directors who expected them to function this way. These chaplains were better trained and served in institutions with a "rehabilitative orientation toward patient care." On the other hand, chaplains who were functioning in an ancillary, limited way had directors who expected them to function in a narrow role. These chaplains reported having poor interpersonal relationships with the professional staff and that their institution tended to be "custodially oriented."[4]

The third obstacle is the lack of facilities, materials, and workers. Of the chaplains surveyed by Lawson, only five schools had chapels. Over half the chaplains reported that the use of general purpose auditoriums and other settings were inadequate as places of worship. Most significantly, the main difficulty which they experienced was the lack of religious education materials designed for use with the retarded. Moreover, most chaplains are dependent upon volunteers from the community to teach the religious education classes. In many institutions only a small proportion of the retardates able to benefit from religious training can be included because of the insufficient number of teachers.

This brief analysis of the obstacles hindering the growth of adequate chaplaincy services to the retarded gives rise to several suggestions regarding new directions to be taken. The most obvious need at this time is a definition of the professional identity of the chaplain who works with mentally retarded persons. Such an identity, defined for clergymen serving in other types of institutions, is relevant for the chaplain of an institution for the retarded. The chaplain, first, is a minister performing a religious ministry. Second, he is a professionally trained person who has submitted himself to supervision through clinical training, developed skills in ministering to persons, and has clinical standards by which to judge the effectiveness of his work.

Like other professional staff members, the chaplain, too, should meet certain qualifications before appointment. These include the basic academic education of the B.A. and B.D. degrees or their equivalent, ordination as a minister, a good standing with his denomination, and endorsement for this special ministry. Pastoral experience and specialized clinical training, at least part of which should be received in an institution for the retarded, are essential. Finally, he should possess personal competence for working with mentally retarded persons. When the chaplain possesses these qualifications, a better relation with the hospital can be established.

A second need is to meaningfully relate the chaplain and the religious ministry to the total institutional program. Acceptance of the chaplaincy service as an integral part of the institution requires recognition of the chaplain as a professionally trained person performing a distinct and unique service. This means that he has a definite place in the administrative structure of the hospital which acknowledges both his training and the uniqueness of his service. The chaplain's responsibility should be clearly defined in the same way that this is done for other staff members. He should be assigned responsibility for the administration of the total religious program. For example, in an institution with a predominately Protestant population and a Protestant chaplain, the chaplain, rather than some other staff member, is responsible for securing and co-ordinating religious services for the Catholic and Jewish residents. Although the chaplain is a member of a specific denomination, his denominational affiliation is not emphasized. He is responsible for the religious care of all the residents, not simply those of his denomination.

As an integral part of the institution staff, he is involved in the interdisciplinary planning staff conferences. The religious ministries to residents, whether religious education or pastoral counseling, must be subject to review by the staff in the same manner that the services of other departments are reviewed. This procedure acknowledges that the religious ministry is part of the total institutional program rather than the personal program of the chaplain.

A third need is for a deeper appreciation of the "context" in which the chaplain functions. Both the role of the chaplain and the nature of the religious ministry are influenced by the environment in which the ministry is set. What may be an excellent program for retarded children in the church may be totally inappropriate for institutionalized retardates. Religious training, therefore, must recognize that these retardates live in an institution, not a home. The gospel must be made relevant to their social experience in the institution. The retardate's personal experience of failure, rejection, and separation from his family must be reconciled. These factors condition his understanding of the Christian faith. Recognition of the context of the ministry assures a religious ministry relevant to the needs of the participants.

Since retardates committed to a state institution are normally full-time residents, the religious ministry is a comprehensive one. This is in contrast to general and mental hospital chaplains whose patient care services are mostly pastoral. The chaplain of an institution for the retarded conducts a broad program of pastoral care, worship, and religious education.

The Role of the Chaplain

The work of the chaplain with institutionalized retardates is, in one sense, no different from the work of the parish minister. The chaplain visits, counsels, comforts, preaches, and teaches. In other respects, however, the work *is* different. The chaplain is identified both as a minister, which defines his unique function, and as a member of the professional staff, which defines his relation to the hospital. The following discussion assumes that the chaplain is clinically trained and accepted as a member of the interdisciplinary staff. The chaplain's role in a residential facility for the mentally retarded includes: (1) administrative functions, (2) pastoral care and counseling, (3) leader of worship, (4) director of religious education, and (5) teaching and research.

Administrative functions.—Administrative functions arise from the chaplain's responsibilities as director of the religious program and his participation in the total hospital program. It is his responsibility to plan and organize a comprehensive and meaningful religious ministry which meets the needs of the residents. Moreover, the Protestant chaplain, if he is the only chaplain, co-ordinates the religious ministry to the Catholic and Jewish residents.

Other administrative duties result from involvement in inter-disciplinary conferences and staff meetings. The work of the chaplain's department at this writer's own institution is an excellent example of what Golden described as an "integrative-co-operative team relationship." The chaplain participates in the diagnostic and disposition conferences and submits a written religious evaluation which becomes part of the resident's permanent record. The religious evaluation includes the resident's religious affiliation, previous religious history before commitment, present level of religious understanding, and recommendations for inclusion in the appropriate religious program. In addition, the chaplain is a member of the Admissions Board which processes applications for admission, the Resident Release Committee which approves discharges from the institution, and the Vocation-Habilitation Board which supervises the habilitation of residents to the community.

Pastoral care and counseling.—The identity of the chaplain is focused most clearly in his ministry to individuals through pastoral care and counseling. Establishing pastoral relationships is essential if the chaplain is to relate the Christian faith to the actual experiences and needs of the retarded. Through personal involvement with individual retardates, the chaplain participates in their daily concerns and problems. He can then offer concrete guidance and counsel.

In these personal ministries, the chaplain embodies the "content" of the worship services and religious education program. Wayne Oates calls this the "symbolic role" of the pastor. Specifically, the chaplain symbolizes love and discipline. Both are major needs of the retarded. The chaplain's entrée to the retarded is simply his willingness to be involved with them and his concern for their problems. Yet, even mentally retarded persons realize that the chaplain is a representative of God and the church. As we shall see later, they identify the chaplain's values with love, respect for other persons, and right behavior. Such a perception of the chaplain's values is a positive asset for retardates struggling to bring their own impulses under control and to find a model with whom to identify. These values and beliefs needed by the retarded cannot be communicated except in a pastoral ministry.

Ministering to the retarded begins at the level of friendship, in informal and unstructured relationships as the chaplain moves among them in the living units, work areas, recreation hall, and infirmary. In visiting new residents, for instance, the chaplain assures them of his personal interest and seeks to allay their anxiety regarding this new experience. His visits to the physically ill in the hospital range from a friendly hello to listening to their feelings about being sick or offering a prayer that God will care for them during this critical time. Other residents often share their good news of a visit home, new clothes, or a special trip or party.

Frequently, the chaplain is sought out for guidance concerning personal problems. A twenty-year-old man stopped the chaplain while walking across the hospital grounds and asked to talk with him. Among Tommy's concerns were conflict with another resident and his own resentment toward being in an institution. In the course of the conversation, however, two more basic problems emerged—inability to control his behavior, i.e., his running off, and his resentment toward his father. In the middle of the interview, Tommy asked:

TOMMY: What did you mean when you read off that paper Sunday about God being like a good father?
CHAPLAIN: What did you think it meant?
TOMMY: It meant that God is good, that he takes care of us, that he wants us to have a good time, and take life easy. He wants us to behave and not get into trouble.
CHAPLAIN: What does this have to do with your problems?
TOMMY: I wish I could see God. But I don't guess I will. I would like to talk with him.
CHAPLAIN: Sometimes we can tell God what we want him to know through other people. Could you tell me what you would like to tell God?
TOMMY: I guess I could. I would like to tell him about my father.
CHAPLAIN: What would you like to tell God about your father?
TOMMY: My father caused me to do all those things I did at home. He shouted at me, threw his shoes at me.

Tommy and the chaplain made an appointment to talk together later in the day in the privacy of the chaplain's office. Together they explored the kind of help Tommy needed to control his behavior and to understand his angry feelings toward his father. Both agreed that Tommy should see one of the social workers for counseling. Tommy's willingness to trust the chaplain with these deeper feelings resulted from a relationship nurtured through numerous informal conversations over an eighteen-month period.

As the preceding conversation indicates, pastoral relationships often move beyond the level of friendship. The chaplain's role as a minister then becomes explicit. One of these pastoral situations is the ministry to the bereaved. Every situation must be handled differently. Yet two "rules of thumb" are usually appropriate in ministering to retarded persons who are bereaved. First, the institutionalized retardate has the right to be told of the death of a family member. When possible, he should attend the funeral or be with the family during this time, depending, of course, upon the retardate and the family situation. Thus he should be told immediately following the death. A delay of several weeks or months only postpones the inevitable bereavement response and often creates hostility and distrust toward the family. Second, the retarded should be told the news honestly, directly, and forthrightly. There is no easy and painless way to tell a person that a family member is dead, but if the wound is made cleanly, it can be healed. Insofar as the chaplain knows, the retarded person should be told the facts surrounding the death, the funeral arrangements, and whether he will be permitted to attend the funeral, and if not, why. In dealing honestly, the chaplain recognizes that the retarded are persons with feelings and that they understand reality. To treat the matter superficially or to deliberately lie denies their basic humanity.

These "rules of thumb" become more meaningful when demonstrated in an actual pastoral conversation of a chaplain with an eighteen-year-old adolescent boy with an IQ of 32. A letter was received from John's mother stating that his father died in November, seven months previously. Since the mother was coming to visit John in two weeks, she wanted someone at the hospital to tell him of his father's death. He had not been told at the time of the death because he could not attend the funeral. The mother felt that this would be upsetting to him.

John was called to his residence hall by an attendant, but he was not told the reason. He was dressed in a white jacket and apron, since he worked in the kitchen. The following conversation took place:

CHAPLAIN: Have a seat, John. I need to talk with you. (*Pause while we both sat down.*) John, we received a letter from your mother. She is coming to see you in two weeks. Has your mother been to see you lately?
JOHN: She came Easter. (*This is not correct.*)
CHAPLAIN: I see. What do you remember about your father?

JOHN: I reckon he is still living.

CHAPLAIN: Your mother wrote about your father. She had some bad news. She told us that your father had died. She wanted someone to tell you about it before she came to see you.

JOHN: He died. *(The news did not seem to make much impact.)*

CHAPLAIN: Yes, John, he died. Your father died several months ago. Your mother did not tell you then because she could not take you to the funeral. She felt that you would be upset to know then if you could not go to the funeral. So, she waited until now.

JOHN: When did he die?

CHAPLAIN: He died last November, about Thanksgiving time. *(Pause)* Do you remember your father?

JOHN: He came to see me a few weeks ago.

CHAPLAIN: It must have been longer ago than that. He died last fall. *(John has difficulty conceptualizing time.)* How do you feel about hearing this news?

JOHN: I feel bad, but not too bad.

CHAPLAIN: It upsets you some but not too much.

JOHN: Um hum.

CHAPLAIN: John, when I tell someone that a member of their family has died, I like to have prayer with them. It helps us to tell God what happened and to ask him to help us. Would you like for us to have prayer together?

JOHN: Yes.

CHAPLAIN: *(We both leaned forward in our chairs, bowed our heads, and closed our eyes.)* Our Father, we thank you that you are our Father and that we can pray to you in times like this. We are thankful that you love and care for us. Would you help John in this time and be with his mother and the other members of his family. We pray in Jesus' name. Amen.

(John continued to hold his head in his hands. He began to cry softly. He wiped his eyes on his apron. I handed him a handkerchief which he took and used to wipe his eyes.)

It's all right for us to cry at times like this. *(Pause)* When someone we love dies, we get upset. That's all right. This is natural. It's good to express our feelings. Don't feel bad about crying or being upset.

JOHN: *(Nodded his head and appeared to have regained his composure.)*

CHAPLAIN: Is there anything you want to ask me?

JOHN: May I go home for a visit? *(I reminded him that his mother was coming to see him in two weeks and that he might ask her about a home visit then. He asked where his father was buried and if his mother was living by herself now. He remembered that before he came to the institution his father had been sick. He drank excessively and a kidney became infected and was removed. John was not permitted to visit his father in the hospital because he was too young. He also wanted to know if he could have a picture of his father, and if he could keep it in the residence hall. I replied that if his mother gave him one, there would be no reason why he could not have it.)*

CHAPLAIN: If you want to, you can stay in the building instead of going back to work. Had you rather stay in the building or go back to work?
JOHN: I would rather go back to work.
CHAPLAIN: You would feel better if you could go back to work?
JOHN: Yes.
CHAPLAIN: All right. If you need to talk with me about this, you let me know and I'll take time to talk with you. Let's go outside and tell Mr. G. *(the attendant)* so he will know what we talked about. I will also go to the kitchen and tell Mrs. M. so that if you do need to return to the building she will understand.

The structured pastoral function of the chaplain also emerges in relation to the religious concerns of residents. For example, William was referred to the chaplain by the building supervisor because he had fought with another resident. They were both punished by being sent to bed. Since that time William has continued to punish himself by refusing to attend church. Physically handicapped, William moves about in a wheelchair. He also has a speech impediment which makes communication difficult.

The chaplain stated that he had missed seeing William in church for the past two Sundays. He wondered where he had been. William replied that he had been punishing himself and thought that Mrs. D. (building supervisor) had told the chaplain. The chaplain replied that Mrs. D. had told him about William's fight with the other resident, but he would like to hear about it from him. He readily described the fight over which television program to watch and of being sent to bed as punishment. Although he had apologized to the other resident he refused to attend church until he could learn to behave. He would continue to punish himself until he could behave.

The chaplain asked William what God wanted us to do when we misbehaved. He said that God wants us to apologize. Even though he had done this, he felt the need to continue to punish himself. Asked why he needed to punish himself, he replied that he wanted to live in the afterlife. He believed that if he were bad he would go down into torment but that if he were good, and if he would behave himself, he would live forever in the life after death.

At this point the chaplain interpreted that God does want us to be good, but he also knows we are only human and that we make mistakes. When we do wrong and are sorry, he forgives us. William asked where this was found in the Bible. The chaplain cited a passage in 1 John which says that if we confess our sins, God will forgive us. Because God does not hold our sins against us, we should not continue to punish ourselves. The chaplain again asked William what God wants us to do when we do wrong. He replied that God wants us to obey, to mind. That means to do right. To obey God means to believe him when he says that our sins are forgiven, replied the chaplain. God does not want us to continue punishing ourselves. Asked how he felt about this, William said this was what C. (a former resident who had been very close to William) told him. The chaplain asked if he could act as though God had forgiven him and stop punishing himself. He could, he replied, and the next Sunday he attended church.

The pastoral function of the chaplain emerges again in the confrontation of residents at the point of their "growing edge." As Cabot and Dicks suggest, growth always involves an element of loss and a gain shown in the realization of a single purpose.[5] The chaplain participates in the pilgrimage of persons who are sloughing off childish and immature ways for more adult and responsible behavior.

As a student chaplain was visiting in a male residence hall, one of the residents asked to talk with him. This request was made shortly after Paul had hit one of the employees. Apparently, this request was motivated by Paul's desire to behave more acceptably in order to avoid jeopardizing his chances for a visit home, scheduled for the following month. Paul was also beginning to feel a need to act like an adult, since he had recently reached his twenty-first birthday.

During eight interviews, Paul expressed several concerns. He was quite anxious about his relationship with his mother because she was the object toward which many of his temper tantrums (when at home) were directed. He was also struggling with the problem: "Should I always expect a reward for being good?" The following excerpts from the second and fourth interviews demonstrate how Paul expressed his concerns and how the student chaplain handled them.

CHAPLAIN: You know you asked me about Jesus last week, Paul.
PAUL: Yeah. I want to know how to believe in Jesus.
CHAPLAIN: Believing what your mother told you about doing to others what you want them to do to you is a good start.
PAUL: Well, I believe that because I love my mother.

CHAPLAIN: Jesus loves you, too, and he wants you to love everybody just as you love your mother.

PAUL: I want to do that but I'm just learning how to be good to people.

CHAPLAIN: You are?

PAUL: Yeah. When I was sixteen years old, I didn't know I could be good. I thought I was meant to act bad. (*He recounts some of his misdeeds.*)

CHAPLAIN: You know now that you can be good.

PAUL: Yes, I think I can. I'm twenty-one years old and I've learned a lot since I come here. I'm not no baby any more. I'm not sixteen now, but I'm twenty-one.

CHAPLAIN: What does it mean to you that you are twenty-one.

PAUL: It means that I gotta be good and do what my supervisor says. I want to do what my mamma wants me to. I'm not going to do anything to hurt my mamma, like the time I got her in the water room and I got her soaking wet and I sprayed her in the face with insect spray.

CHAPLAIN: Do you know why you did those things to your mamma, Paul?

PAUL: I just didn't know no better. I was just a young teen-ager and I thought it was fun. But I know a lot different now. I'm twenty-one years old. I've learned a lot. I'm here with all the other boys and away from my mamma because of the way I acted and all those things I did. I know that. All those things put me in here and I hope the things I do now will put me out of here.

CHAPLAIN: You'd rather be out?

PAUL: Sure I would. That's why I want to be good, and I want to go home. Have you got a calendar, Preacher G.?

CHAPLAIN: You're ready to go home any time.

PAUL: I sure am, and I don't want to cause no trouble. I heard Preacher S. read a story out of the Bible last Sunday. It said God wanted you to obey those people who were trying to help you. Is that what I should do, Preacher G.? Just tell me what you think.

The pastoral function of the chaplain often involves long-term counseling in a structured relationship. In a state institution, oriented toward rehabilitation, several disciplines work therapeutically with individuals and groups. Counseling assignments are usually made on the nature of the presenting problem of the resident. The counselor's ability to work with a particular person is also considered. With many retardates the religious role of the chaplain is an asset.

A twenty-eight-year-old white male resident (IQ 52) was seen for counseling because of frequent behavior problems. Over the past few years he had often run away from the institution, fought with other residents, and stole. He was first admitted at eight years of age for two months, readmitted at age fourteen, and has resided in the institution since. His irresponsible behavior and limited use of his right hand prevented his inclusion in the educational and

vocational training program. However, the placement officer felt
that James could do limited work in a carefully supervised situation.

Since the chaplain had previously talked with James in regard to
other misconduct, it was easy to initiate a formal counseling relationship. The chaplain simply stated that he was concerned about
the trouble James was continually in and would like to talk with
him about this. Although the interviews were carefully structured
as to time and purpose, no counseling objectives were formed until
after the first three interviews. Three problems quickly emerged.

First, it was apparent that James was quite immature, demanded
immediate gratification of impulses, and related to other persons in
an extractive and manipulative way. For instance, he insisted on
being first in the lunch line, pushed other residents out of his way,
and would strike them when upset. Second, it seemed that part
of his behavior problems could be attributed to boredom and lack
of purpose. In the first interview he expressed a desire for a job
in the institutional work program. This seemed to be important to
him. Third, his family was inconsistent in their treatment of him.
They often went several weeks or months without writing or visiting, though they lived close by. This neglect upset him to the point
that he frequently threatened to misbehave if he did not hear from
them, and he often did.

Subsequently, it was decided that the long-range goal would be
to prepare James for a job in the institutional work program. James
was frankly told that his behavior would determine whether or not
he was given the assignment. After three months both the chaplain
and James would evaluate his behavior in the residence hall and
decide his readiness for the job.

During the interviews, conducted twice weekly for forty-five
minutes each, James was free to discuss any problems or concerns.
He talked freely and with some insight. His concerns centered
around his relationships with other residents and employees, his
family, and his desire for a job. Consequently, the chaplain was
reflective, seeking to help James to be honest about his feelings,
but at the same time representing reality to him. For example, between the first and second interview, James struck with his fist
another resident who accidentally kicked him. In exploring the events
preceding the episode, he said that he was already mad about
several things. When kicked, he turned his anger against the other
resident. In discussing other incidents in which he was angry and

abusive, it was apparent that he had precipitated them by his unreasonable demands. With each of these incidents the chaplain led James to restructure the event and to pinpoint the ways in which he was responsible for their occurring.

Although religion was seldom mentioned, the identity of the chaplain as a minister was clearly maintained. On several occasions, James commented that a preacher wanted people to be good and live right. The identification of the minister with the "superego" was not discouraged because James's greatest need was to bring his impulses under control. However, it was reinterpreted in terms of the chaplain's desire that James become a trustworthy person, that he become a "working boy" by being more responsible for his actions, and that he learn to respect the rights of others.

Over the three-month period, James's behavior improved, probably because of his motivation for a job and the privileges accompanying it. As previously agreed, he was referred to the vocational placement officer for job assignment. Before placement on the farm, he was carefully instructed as to the requirements of the job and informed that his continued placement depended upon his behavior. For two months James worked on the farm and presented no serious management problems. However, one morning he became upset and left his assignment without permission. Although removed from the assignment, he had demonstrated his ability to modify his behavior when properly motivated.

In essence, the pastoral ministry of the chaplain to individual retardates is a concrete symbol of the love and discipline of the Christian gospel. He symbolizes the concern of God for every person and the requirements of God that we love our neighbor as ourselves. In more formal and structured ways, however, through worship and religious education, the chaplain also ministers to the religious needs of institutionalized retardates.

Worship.—Sunday worship services are significant events in the life of institutionalized retardates. Since many attended church at home and others will return to the community later, the worship service is similar to community church services. The purpose of the service is to lead the residents in the worship of God through the use of music, Bible reading, prayer, affirmation of faith, and sermon. Though well structured, the service involves movement from one activity to another. Attention is never focused on one activity for a long period of time. All participate through singing, saying the Lord's Prayer in unison, and reciting the affirmation of faith. Selected residents participate more specifically through singing in the choir, reading the Bible, and leading in prayer.

Through the songs, prayers, and Bible readings, the residents both worship God and learn about the Christian faith. Even in the worship service, the chaplain is a pastor and teacher, as well as a leader of worship, often explaining the meaning of worship, prayer, and the Bible. The best opportunity for teaching is in the sermon.[6] Though brief and usually limited to one point, the sermon relates the teachings of the Bible to life situations. In interpreting the life situations of the retarded, the chaplain is informed by his pastoral ministry. Thus the Christian faith is presented as story, event, and personalities, not as abstract doctrine. The dynamic qualities contained in the story, such as love, hope, faith, obedience, and courage, are related to the life of the residents.

One Sunday a chaplain preached on "Finding a New Family." Based on Jesus' separation from his family at the beginning of his ministry, recorded in Mark 3:31-35, the sermon emphasized that every person must leave home to make a new home for himself. Thus their leaving home is similar to the experience of almost everyone, including the chaplain. While we cannot return home, we can find a new family among the residents and employees of the hospital. Even away from home, God continues to love and care for us. While visiting in one of the residence halls the next morning, the chaplain was approached by a young man. After several years of residence at the hospital, he was still quite resentful toward his family and the hospital for placing him there. Remarking that he had heard the sermon yesterday, he guessed that the chaplain was right, that it was natural to leave home. He would have to make the best of it.

In addition to the Sunday services for the entire institution population, weekday worship services are often held in the separate residence halls. These are necessary for the physically handicapped and severely retarded who cannot participate in the Sunday service. At this writer's institution, for instance, a weekly worship service is conducted for approximately twenty-five severely retarded, physically handicapped persons. They come in wheelchairs to the dining room where "church" is held. Only a few have any speech, but they enjoy the music, the prayers, the Bible reading, the pictures, and the "sermon."

The regular worship program is enriched by a special emphasis on the holidays of Christmas, Easter, and Thanksgiving. Thanksgiving is observed by a special service on Thanksgiving morning, and Easter is celebrated by a sunrise service, held out-of-doors. To symbolize the event, three crosses, facing the east, are set in the background. In recognition of the significance of the day, a guest minister from the community is invited to deliver the sermon.

The sacramental aspect of worship is not well developed among Protestant chaplains at this time. Both chaplains and residents represent a wide range of denominations with differing policies regarding the administration of baptism and the Lord's Supper. However, some do conduct regular communion or Lord's Supper services. One chaplain has a monthly communion service for the residents who have been baptized.

Religious education.—Institutionalized retardates usually remain in the institution for life, or at least for several years while receiving education and vocational training. These persons desire religious knowledge and ask religious questions. A full religious ministry must include a program of religious education, organized by small classes, and geared to the appropriate educational and developmental level. Responsibility for the religious care of several hundred persons means that the chaplain is more often a supervisor or coordinator of other teachers than a teacher himself.

Chapter 5 presented in detail a philosophy of Christian education applicable to any group of retardates. It is necessary here to note only two of the problems involved in a religious education program for institutionalized retardates. The first is the lack of curriculum materials designed for use with retarded persons. Denominational or nondenominational materials created for normal children are most commonly adapted. However, there are two drawbacks to this material. One is its orientation toward middle class family life. Institutionalized retardates do not live in families, and illustrations and activities emphasizing family life are inappropriate. Second, this material does not recognize the retarded's personal experiences of failure and rejection which too often result in apathy, hostility, distrust, and estrangement.

In adapting these materials it is necessary to anticipate the possible response of the students. The following questions may be helpful. What past experiences does the student bring to this lesson? How can they be utilized to relate this lesson to his life? What emotional responses are these concepts and ideas likely to elicit? For example, the concept of God as a good father may be met with a negative response from a person who has never known a good father. The Christian life may be presented in such a way as to appear sentimental or unrealistic in the mistaken assumption that it is easy for the retarded to be "Christian." One adult man frequently comments that "it isn't easy to be a Christian around here. You're just wasting your time preaching to these people, Chaplain." How does the lesson apply to the student's present situation in the institution? What areas of his life are touched? A lesson on Jesus in the Temple, illustrating the problem of authority and responsibility, is applicable to the student's relationship to authority persons in the institution. His responsibility for obeying the rules governing his privilege of moving about the grounds without an employee escort can also be discussed in the context of this story.

In a few instances chaplains have written their own curriculum. Perhaps the most creative and promising work is that of Chaplain S. Willard Agee of the Polk State School, Polk, Pennsylvania. Agee developed a research type curriculum for the "Christian Character Education of the Mentally Retarded." Religious education for the mentally retarded, Agee hypothesized, should involve three aspects: "the teaching of content, the structuring of mentally healthy and Christian attitudes, and the development of Christian social skills."[7] Believing that retardates could tell their level of Christian character efficiency and their basic instructional needs, indirect and projective techniques were used to test some aspects of the Christian Character Education program. The program consists of "two units of content-teaching followed with promotion into one of several skill-fellowship groups."

The second problem in developing a religious education program is the lack of trained teachers. Here the chaplain becomes a teacher of teachers—recruiting, training, and supervising volunteer teachers from community churches or colleges. At one institution, for instance, Thursday night is set aside for religious education. Teachers from the community churches conduct small classes for a forty-five-minute session. At the Clover Bottom Hospital and School, students from four neighboring colleges conduct several classes for residents enrolled in the school program and the vocational training program. Prior to the first class meeting, the students participate in an intensive orientation program.

As state institutions become more community oriented, community churches are beginning to provide religious training in their churches for retardates affiliated with their denomination. At Clover Bottom, fifteen carefully selected residents attend Sunday school classes and worship services at four community churches. Transportation and supervision are provided by the local church. The residents are taught in separate classes in some churches and integrated into regular classes in others. Many have been baptized and accepted as members of the church. Such a program provides religious training in a "church" setting.

Teaching and research.—As a member of the professional staff, the chaplain participates in the hospital teaching and research program. This dimension of the chaplain's role has too seldom been recognized either by chaplains themselves or by hospital administrators. The chaplain, however, is as responsible as any other staff member for training workers and furthering the growing body of knowledge in mental retardation.

One of the teaching functions is with the general teaching program of the hospital. In training programs for psychiatric aides who work directly with residents, the chaplain interprets his role in the hospital, the religious concerns and needs of the retarded which the aide is likely to encounter, and the ministry to the bereaved and dying. Another teaching program is offered to medical students from a neighboring medical college. Included in the sessions is a round-table discussion on counseling the parents of retarded children. As a member of this panel, the writer has used the interviews presented in chapter 3 to illustrate the parents' emotional involvement, the problems of management, the theological concerns, and the clergyman's role in ministering to the parents.

A second teaching task is the training of religious educators, pastors, and Sunday school teachers in the principles and methods of religious training for the retarded. Persons such as religious educators, serving local churches or denominational education boards, may teach classes in the institution in order to learn how to work with the retarded through firsthand experience. A popular method for teaching pastors at many institutions is an annual "Clergy Day." Lectures and discussions usually evolve around the nature of mental retardation, the treatment and management of the retarded, and the role of the church in the care of the retarded and their families.

A third teaching program is clinical pastoral education. Ministers and/or ministerial students spend a designated period at the institution under the supervision of an accredited chaplain supervisor. Although several accredited supervisors are currently offering programs, clinical pastoral education in this setting is still in the exploratory stages. Of the issues still to be resolved, the most pressing seems to be the purpose of clinical training. Is clinical training in an institution for the retarded to be regarded as the beginning clinical course such as is given in other settings? Is it to be designed solely to teach ministers to work with mentally retarded persons and their families? The setting does determine to some degree the nature of the program. Yet, there seems to be no reason why clinical pastoral education in a hospital for the retarded could not be included in the theological curriculum as a beginning clinical course alongside the courses in general and mental hospitals. In this setting, the student also has opportunity to study the history of and dynamic factors in specific cases, to develop helpful pastoral relationships, and to examine his own pattern of relatedness and emotional needs which block an effective ministry.

Significant contributions by chaplains should be made through research and writing. Of all the functions of the chaplain, his responsibility for conducting research is the least recognized. Both as a professionally trained person and as a representative of the church, the chaplain is obligated to contribute to the growing body of literature on mental retardation. Currently, chaplains have produced research in such areas as Christian education curriculum, teacher training, Bible knowledge of the retarded, and the minister's role in mental retardation.

These studies, however, are only suggestive of the kinds of research that chaplains should be producing. Chaplains are in a strategic position to contribute to the development of a religious ministry to the retarded in the community as well as in the institution. At this point denominational and interdenominational agencies with educational responsibilities for the retarded need to recognize the research potential of chaplains. Areas of co-operative study should include the religious development of the retarded, experimental religious education curriculum, and the pastoral care of the retarded and their families. Such collaboration would, we would hope, break through the redundancy that characterizes the current writing in this field and lead to a more profound and realistic understanding of the religious needs of mentally retarded persons.

In summary then, the church is responsible for the religious care of institutionalized retardates. This ministry should be rendered by a clinically trained clergyman, employed full time by the hospital and functioning in an "integrative-co-operative team relationship." There is a marked increase in the number of full-time chaplains, and the work of these men, in many instances, preceded the current concern of the church for the mentally retarded. Several needs still exist, however. Among these are the need for greater clarity regarding the professional identity of the chaplain, his role in the religious care of institutionalized retardates, and his teaching and research responsibility to enrich the ministry of the whole church to mentally retarded persons.

Notes

1. Donald W. Lawson, "Religious Programs for the Mentally Retarded Residing in Institutions," *American Journal of Mental Deficiency,* November, 1961, pp. 459-63.
2. After this chapter was written, a definition of chaplaincy services and standards appeared in "Standards for State Residential Institutions for the Mentally Retarded," Monograph Supplement, *American Journal of Mental Deficiency,* January, 1964, pp. 48-49, 78. These standards should be influential in the development of more adequate chaplaincy services and in the employment of clinically trained chaplains. However, it will likely be several years before these standards become normative.
3. Edward S. Golden, "What Influences the Role of the Protestant Chaplain in an Institutional Setting?" *The Journal of Pastoral Care,* Winter, 1962, pp. 218-25.
4. *Ibid.,* p. 220.
5. Richard C. Cabot and Russell L. Dicks, *The Art of Ministering to the Sick* (New York: The Macmillan Co., 1955), pp. 375-76.
6. An excellent example of a sermon preached to mentally retarded persons by Sigurd Petersen is found in *Pastoral Preaching,* ed. Charles F. Kemp (St. Louis: The Bethany Press, 1963), pp. 164-70. Petersen has also included orders of worship for a children's service and a youth service in *Retarded Children: God's Children,* pp. 150-52.
7. J. Willard Agee, "Through the Church Year with the Mentally Retarded: A Program of Christian Character Education" (Polk, Pa: Polk State School, 1961), p. 1, mimeographed. See also, J. Willard Agee, "Lest the Least Be Lost: Character Education of the Retarded," *American Journal of Mental Deficiency,* November, 1958, pp. 490-94.

8

The Social Welfare Role
of the Church

Increasing recognition is now being given to the church's responsibility for providing and pioneering social welfare services for the
mentally retarded and their families. Among Protestants, the Lutherans have taken this responsibility most seriously. They sponsor
several residential facilities for the retarded, while the General
Association of Regular Baptists is presently constructing a facility
for residential care. More responsible social welfare ministries, however, await the recognition that mental retardation is a social problem requiring a broad approach by all social institutions. Some of
the ramifications of mental retardation which necessitate special
professional personnel and services were discussed in detail in chapters 2 and 3. Requiring attention now is the enlargement of the
church's social outreach to include mental retardation. Responsible and immediate action to provide or pioneer needed services
within the church's province is clearly indicated.

Locus of Responsibility

Responsibility for implementing a social welfare ministry is not
restricted to any one level of the denomination, although a specific
agency or commission may be assigned to develop and encourage
services. The impetus may emerge from either the local church or
from a denominational agency. Yet, the variety of services which
the mentally retarded need requires the co-operation of all levels
of the denomination—national, regional, and local.

In the Methodist church, the initiative has been taken by the
Board of Hospitals and Homes. Specific plans developed for a welfare ministry have not yet received the endorsement of the church

and so have not been implemented. Olin E. Oeschger, the general secretary of the Board, suggests that future action by the Methodists should follow three lines. First, he urges the establishment of a national agency for the care of severely retarded children to be closely supervised by the Board of Hospitals and Homes. Second, a more adequate health and welfare ministry should be developed in the local church, including day care programs, homemaker services, and sheltered workshops. Finally, the annual conferences should expand the services of existing institutions to include the mentally retarded.[1]

In the General Association of Regular Baptist Churches, the impetus originated in a young married couples' class in the Garfield Avenue Baptist Church of Milwaukee. Their interest resulted from an experience with a mongoloid child. Upon discovering the overwhelming need for facilities and services, they organized a committee to advance opportunities for the placement and training of the mentally retarded. In 1958, the committee incorporated under the name of "Shepherds, Inc." Later it received the approval of the GARBC. Resulting from the work of this committee is a residential facility for the care of the mentally retarded and the development of special Sunday school classes and day schools.

In the Lutheran Church—Missouri Synod—the task of "promoting and co-ordinating various efforts in the field of mental retardation as it relates particularly to the Lutheran parents of retarded, other lay members, teachers, and pastors" has been centered in "The Commission on Mental Retardation." The Commission, related to the Division of Social Action and Welfare, is composed of a small group of pastors, teachers, and lay persons, appointed by the president of the Synod. Responsibilities involve determining the current needs and adequacy of present services and educating the general church membership with the role of the church in mental retardation. Two institutes geared to Sunday school teachers, schoolteachers, and pastors, are currently conducted each year.

Although all levels of the denomination are involved in the welfare ministry to the mentally retarded, a division of responsibility is often necessary. The functions of denominational boards and commissions consist of determining the nature and extent of services needed, of educating local churches regarding the problem of mental retardation, and of guiding in the development of services by local churches or by associations of churches in a specific geographical region. Local churches and associations of churches should also assume responsibility for assessing the present services provided for the retarded in their community and for creating welfare ministries not otherwise available. Specifically, such a ministry should include church-sponsored community services for the retarded residing at home, residential care for the retarded who, for various reasons, must be removed from their home, and the promotion of responsible legislation and social action by the local, state, and national governments.

Church-Sponsored Community Services

Many local and state governments are either unable or unwilling to provide adequate special services for the retarded. In many instances, local churches have creatively provided otherwise unavailable services or have supplemented existing programs through volunteer participation.

One area of crucial need in most communities is day care centers. Day care programs accomplish a double purpose. Parents are freed from the burden of twenty-four-hour supervision of the child so that they may maintain a fairly normal social life. At the same time, the child receives educational, social, and recreational opportunities geared to the appropriate level of development. One church, for instance, simply allowed a parent organization to use its facilities for a day care center during the week without charge. The parent group assumed complete responsibility for the organization and maintenance of the program. Other churches have taken the initiative in beginning and supervising such a program.

On Tuesday afternoons, the First Methodist Church of Wausau, Wisconsin, sponsors an "opportunity group" for physically and mentally handicapped children in the community. About fourteen children presently attend, twelve of whom come from other churches. "The purpose of these Tuesday afternoon sessions," stated one of the church workers, "is to promote better social adjustment through stories, games, music, art, and field trips. We hope to develop in the children some good activities and habits, and to bring them kindness and love."[2]

Similarly, the Calvary Baptist Church of Jackson, Mississippi, sponsors a "Spend the Day" one day a week for mentally retarded persons. The church gym serves as the center for a program of arts and crafts. Also, another activity which a church could effectively sponsor is a Teen Town or a Scout troop for adolescent retardates.

An urgent need also exists for full-time centers staffed by professionally trained workers. Such centers provide educational opportunities for retarded children either too young or too severely retarded to participate in the public school special education classes. This type of program is similar to a regular kindergarten. Since little or no academic training is possible, the emphasis is on social experience and the development of self-help skills, designed to assist the child in becoming as self-sufficient as possible.

An example of this type of program is the day care center in Nashville, Tennessee, jointly sponsored by the Protestant Orphanage Foundation and the Davidson County Council for Retarded Children. While continuing its work with orphaned and neglected children, the Foundation enlarged its scope of ministry to include retarded children. No public supported day care program was available in Davidson County. Present plans call for the Foundation to assume complete responsibility for the operation of the center in order to free the Council to pioneer additional community services for the retarded.

A second type of church-sponsored community service, special education classes, is similar to day care programs. Many school systems recognize their obligation to provide special classes for the retarded. Inadequate provisions by some systems deprive many retarded persons of any formal education at all. Protestant churches, therefore, should seriously consider their responsibility to pioneer educational opportunities for the retarded when the public schools are unable or unwilling to do so.

Under the direction of its pastor, A. Richard Smith, the Trinity Lutheran Church of Tullahoma, Tennessee, did just that.[3] The public school system provided special classes for the educable retarded but was unable to extend these classes to the trainable retarded. The county Association for Retarded Children was also stymied in its efforts. At this point, the Trinity Lutheran Church entered the picture. Offering to furnish the facilities and equipment and to provide a teacher, the church challenged the county Association to provide the money for the teacher's salary.

The school began in September of 1958, with six students enrolled. The children learned social adjustment through fellowship with other boys and girls who were their emotional and mental equals. They played group games and helped one another at mealtime with their table manners. They learned to care for their personal needs, such as buttoning clothing, tying shoes, and toilet-training. They studied academic subjects, learning to recognize objects, words, and money. And for the first time, many of these children received religious training. They learned prayers, Bible verses, and stories from the Bible.

State and local school funds were finally made available. In recognition of the school's achievement, the local school system asked the Trinity Lutheran Trainable School, incorporated as a joint function of the Trinity congregation and the county Association, to continue the school's operation. In 1963, however, the operation of the school was turned over to the local school system.

A third community service is participation in homemaker services. On a regular basis, a worker visits in the home of a family with a retarded child. Her purpose is to give the mother companionship, to assist in the management of the child, or to care for the child while the mother shops, participates in recreational activities, or performs chores away from the home. Homemaker services, sponsored by public welfare departments, parent organizations, or other community agencies, often utilize volunteer workers. This type of service could easily be provided by a church for its members who have retarded children. The ladies in a Sunday school class or missionary society could, on a rotating basis, care for the retarded child a day or half day weekly, allowing the mother freedom to attend weekday church activities or simply to enjoy a period of leisure time.

A final area of service is volunteer participation in special education classes in the public schools, day care centers, and residential facilities. Volunteers are probably most widely used in state institutions to supplement existing activities and to staff new programs for which hospital employees are unavailable. In one state institution, volunteers direct the art club, work with the choir, assist teachers in the educational program, and provide an escort service for residents unable to move about the grounds unaccompanied. Sunday school classes and missionary organizations give parties in the residence halls, especially during the Christmas and Easter holiday seasons. One missionary society "adopted" two female residents for a year. They visited the residents at the hospital, secured clothing for them, remembered them on their birthday and holidays, and took them for visits to their homes.

Most of these services are clearly within the province of local churches. They can be accomplished without an extensive outlay of money or personnel. Such ministries, however, give concrete and visible expression to the church's missionary concern. Establishment of personal relationships with the persons served is the basic means of missionary outreach. Almost as significant as the ministry itself is the possibility that the church's involvement in direct services to these persons may serve to alert others to the needs of the retarded and their families.

Residential Care

A more costly and far-reaching aspect of the church's welfare ministry is the provision of church-sponsored residential care facilities or foster homes. A small percentage of mentally retarded persons must be removed from their homes. Sporadic attempts to provide for the retarded have been made by various organizations of the church. For example, the Bishop of Myra in the fourth century is reported to have had compassion on them and urged giving them tender care. In the sixteenth century, St. Vincent de Paul and his "Sisters of Charity" gave kind treatment to the retarded whom they brought under their care in the Bicetre. The Institutes of Justinian provided caretakers for the retarded as well as for the deaf and dumb. One Byzantine nunnery cared for the sick and idiotic. At Gheel, in Brabant, a religious shrine was established where both the insane and the retarded were cared for in private homes.

In spite of these commendable efforts, the church's concern for the retarded has never approached its efforts between 1860 and 1920 to care for dependent children. Nor does it approach current programs to provide residential care for the aged or retired. Finding some form of residential care for retarded persons is a tremendous need. How the church may help meet it is worthy of as much consideration as we have given to other social problems.

In at least three ways churches can furnish residential services for the mentally retarded. The most obvious first step is to expand present church welfare ministries to include the mentally retarded. In some situations, this is already being done, but usually unintentionally. For example, Olin Oeschger has reported a study of Methodist agencies for children and youth. Some mildly retarded children were being served, not usually because of the retardation, but because of family situations and other problems. Moreover, this writer's observation is that many church-related orphanages that inadvertently admit retarded children feel unprepared to care for them. Usually they are transferred to what is described as "a more appropriate facility," meaning a state institution.

Church-related agencies serving children and youth, however, can adequately care for the mentally retarded. Mildly retarded persons, in many instances, can be integrated into regular programs and living arrangements. The moderately or severely retarded would require a separate cottage or dormitory. Admittedly, this transition, would necessitate a careful study of mental retardation, special training of cottage parents and other workers, and acceptance of limited developmental goals. Yet, extension of present facilities to serve the mentally retarded can be done if the church has the heart and will. Hindering this extension is the apparent belief that the retarded are not our responsibility.

A second step is the establishment of residential facilities for the exclusive care of the mentally retarded. For instance, some institutions with a program for normal children have found a decreasing number of children needing this particular type care. Thus, in 1954, the Vasa Children's Home at Red Wing, Minnesota, operated by the Minnesota Conference, Augustana Lutheran Church, changed its function from caring for "orphaned" children to the mentally retarded. About fifty children, ambulatory and nonambulatory, with IQs below fifty, are currently served.

When impractical to convert existing institutions, new ones should be built. Of the major Protestant bodies the Lutherans have been most responsive to the need for church-sponsored residential facilities for the retarded. They currently sponsor several homes; one is the Good Shepherd Home at Terra Bella, California, with a resident population of 115 and a property valuation of $569,134. As of 1963, there were 286 retarded persons waiting to be admitted as soon as a vacancy occurs. Similar institutions report large waiting lists. This is a chronic problem with almost every public institution for the retarded.

The most important single factor in developing a residential facility is the desire to do so rather than the size or resources of the denomination. The present work of the General Association of Regular Baptist Churches demonstrates this. One Sunday school class's vision that the care of the mentally retarded was a missionary responsibility of the church became the vision of the entire GARB.

Financed largely through love offerings from churches, Vacation Bible schools, and interested individuals, a facility is under construction at Union Grove, Wisconsin. This, indeed, has been a venture of faith, born out of a vision and nurtured by a conviction that mental retardation is the church's business.

A third step is the provision of foster homes by local churches and individual church members. Less than 5 per cent of the total mentally retarded population in the United States reside in institutions. Many of these persons committed to institutions could have remained in the community or could now return to the community if suitable foster homes were available. To meet this problem, churches, first of all, should encourage qualified persons to serve as foster parents— caring for retarded children, adolescents, and adults in their own home. This would allow childless couples in particular to find fulfilment through being "parents." In itself this is a significant Christian vocation. Co-operation with the Department of Public Welfare or an appropriate private agency would be essential, however. For instance, a mildly retarded woman of forty-five, resident of a state institution for several years, was given a work placement in the home of a family who cared for the wife's mother. This woman shared in the care of the elderly mother and in the housework. Moreover, she was accepted as a "member" of the family, participating in their social and religious life. She has been warmly received by the church where the family attends and was recently accepted as a member.

Local churches should also explore the possibility of developing community foster homes. A civic club, for instance, adopted this as a club project. With the co-operation of the county Association for Retarded Children, a large home was built and a couple selected to be foster parents to several retarded persons who, for various reasons, needed to be removed or had already been removed from their home. A food and clothing allowance for each child was paid and a stipend given to the foster parents. Many churches already provide similar services for dependent children. This service could easily be extended to include the mentally retarded.

In essence, the church's role in providing residential or foster home care for mentally retarded persons is similar to its role in ministering to dependent children. An important exception to this general principle is that the severely and moderately retarded require care and supervision throughout their entire life.

Promotion of Legislation and Social Action

Providing direct services is only one aspect of the church's role. Most services will continue to be given by various governmental and private agencies. The adequacy of these, however, depends upon responsible legislation and social action. Unfortunately, the prophetic voice calling attention to the plight of the mentally retarded and their families has not been the church's voice. Instead, the prophets have been the National Association for Retarded Children and related local parent organizations, the American Association on Mental Deficiency, a few enlightened state governments, and the Federal Government, motivated by the personal interest of the late President Kennedy.

Intelligent and resourceful action is possible only if the churches are informed. Recognizing the need for a simple but basic guide, the Division of Christian Education of the National Council of Churches commissioned Dr. Charles E. Palmer to write a manual on *The Church and the Exceptional Person*, published by Abingdon Press in 1961. Written in nontechnical language, the book contains chapters on the classification and description of types of exceptionality, how to locate "exceptional persons," how to prepare the church to accept them, how to minister to them both in and outside the church, and the church's responsibility for co-operating with the community. This book can be used individually by interested laymen or as the basis for a churchwide study.

Such a study was sponsored by the Commission on Missions of the Methodist Church in 1963. Study manuals on ministering to "persons of special needs" were prepared. To supplement this material and to acquaint the church with local resources, one suburban church invited representatives of various community agencies to speak. When the superintendent of a state hospital and school for the retarded, located in the same suburb as the church, discussed the limited budget which prevented adding services desperately needed, the church members were appalled. They pledged their support in working toward increased funds for the mentally retarded. Similarly, the Nazarene Ministerial Association in a metropolitan community invited representatives, including this writer, from local social welfare agencies to speak at their monthly luncheon meetings. These ministers received immediate information and guidance in ministering to persons with special problems in their own congregations. Resource persons and agencies to whom they could turn for assistance in handling these specific problems in the future were also identified. Moreover, a Baptist church used the period following the Wednesday night fellowship supper to acquaint its members with the problems of mental retardation. A member of the church, supervisor of special education in the public schools, served as the resource person.

Education of the church membership regarding the problems associated with mental retardation is basic to responsible social action. Churches have been more active in providing welfare services for the retarded than in promoting responsible legislation and social action, however. Both the provision of direct services and the promotion of such services by society are necessary. The church as a social institution and individual church members as citizens should work toward the development of reasonable community services for the mentally retarded and their families. Specific areas where church support is needed include community diagnostic and evaluation centers, day care programs for the severely retarded, special classes in the public schools for the moderately and mildly retarded, vocation-habilitation services, additional residential facilities and increased funds for existing ones, research programs regarding the medical, educational, psychological, and social dimensions of mental retardation, training of professional personnel, and more adequate dissemination of information to the general public.

In its social welfare role the church champions the right of this neglected minority to have adequate care and treatment through services provided by the community and the church. Underlying this concern is the belief that only concrete services which meet the needs of the whole man are adequate manifestations of the church's missionary and social responsibility.

Notes

1. Olin E. Oeschger, "Retarded Children: How the Church Can Help," *Together*, November, 1963, p. 30.
2. *Ibid.*
3. A. Richard Smith, "Impetuous Venture in Tullahoma," *Resource*, April, 1960, pp. 6-8.

Bibliography

A complete listing of books, journal articles, pamphlets, and unpublished papers on "religion and religious education of the mentally retarded" is maintained by the National Association for Retarded Children, Inc., 386 Park Avenue South, New York 16, New York, and can be obtained by request. For persons interested in the latest trends and research from the behavioral sciences, the following journals should be consulted: *American Journal of Mental Deficiency, Exceptional Children, Mental Retardation, Social Casework,* and *Social Work.*

The following list of carefully selected books and articles is intended as a guide for readers desiring to explore in greater depth the nature of mental retardation and the ministry of the church.

The Church and Mental Retardation

BOGARDUS, LADONNA. *Christian Education of Retarded Children and Youth.* Nashville: Abingdon Press, 1963.
   The first book length treatment of the subject, offering concrete suggestions on the objectives and methods of Christian education for retarded persons. Highly recommended.
FOSHEE, HOWARD. "Your Church and the Mentally Retarded." Nashville, Tenn.: Baptist Sunday School Board.
KEMP, CHARLES F. *The Church: The Gifted and Retarded Child.* St. Louis: Bethany Press, 1957.
   An introductory work—helpful, but limited by the absence of case material.
PALMER, CHARLES E. *The Church and the Exceptional Person.* Nashville: Abingdon Press, 1961.
   An excellent introduction to the church's ministry to exceptional persons, including the mentally retarded.
PETERSEN, SIGURD D. *Retarded Children: God's Children.* Philadelphia: Westminster Press, 1960.
   A perceptive book by a Lutheran minister with intensive experience with the retarded pictures the retarded as persons with religious needs and relates Christian theology to the problem of retardation.

STUBBLEFIELD, HAROLD W. "The Ministry and Mental Retardation," *Journal of Religion and Health,* January, 1964.
A report of an exploratory survey of the ministry of 220 clergymen to mentally retarded persons and their parents.

_____. "The Church and Mental Retardation," *Pastoral Psychology,* September, 1962.
A special issue devoted exclusively to mental retardation and containing new material on pastoral care of the retarded and their parents.

WILLIAMSON, MARGARET (ed.). *Concern and Response. The Report of the Second National Conference on the Churches and Social Welfare.* New York: Friendship Press, 1962.
An overview of the church's social welfare responsibility with a section on mental retardation containing suggestions which need immediate implementation.

The Nature of Mental Retardation

DAVIES, STANLEY POWELL. *The Mentally Retarded in Society.* New York: Columbia University Press, 1959.
A historical study of social attitudes toward the retarded.

DOLL, EUGENE E. "A Historical Survey of Research and Management of Mental Retardation in the United States," *Readings on the Exceptional Child: Research and Theory.* Edited by E. PHILIP TRAPP and PHILIP HIMELSTEIN. New York: Appleton-Century-Crofts, Inc., 1962.

HEBER, RICK. "Mental Retardation: Concept and Classification," *ibid.*
An authoritative discussion of the current concept and classification of mental retardation as accepted by the American Association on Mental Deficiency.

MASLAND, RICHARD L., SARASON, SEYMOUR B., and GLADWIN, THOMAS. *Mental Subnormality: Biological, Psychological, and Cultural Factors.* New York: Basic Books, Inc., 1958.
An excellent survey of the current understanding of the biological, psychological, and cultural aspects of mental retardation.

The Family and Mental Retardation

BUCK, PEARL S. *The Child Who Never Grew.* New York: The John Day Company, 1950.
An honest, realistic account of one mother's response to a retarded child. Appropriate for parents.

FARBER, BERNARD. "Effects of a Severely Mentally Retarded Child on the Family." *Readings on the Exceptional Child: Research and Theory.*
A summary of several studies by the author which gives the minister concrete evidence of the family's response to a retarded child as influenced by, among other factors, social class and religious affiliation.

FRENCH, EDWARD L., and SCOTT, J. CLIFFORD. *Child in the Shadows: A Manual for Parents of Retarded Children.* New York: J. B. Lippincott, 1960.
A book for parents seeking information, but can also be read with profit by religious workers.

MURRAY, MRS. MAX A. "Needs of Parents of Mentally Retarded Children," *American Journal of Mental Deficiency*. Vol. 63, May, 1959.
Parents' need for help with the theological crisis which the birth of a retarded child creates is given special attention.

OATES, WAYNE E. *The Religious Dimensions of Personality*. New York: Association Press, 1957.
A significant discussion of, among other topics, the religious dimensions of man's heredity and birth, with specific attention to mental retardation.

STACEY, CHALMERS L., and DeMARTINO, MANFRED F. *Counseling and Psychotherapy with the Mentally Retarded*. Glencoe, Illinois: The Free Press, 1957.
A collection of articles dealing not only with counseling and psychotherapy but also with other therapeutic methods such as group therapy, play therapy, psychodrama, speech therapy, and vocational-occupational-industrial therapy. Also contains excellent articles on counseling with parents.

ABOUT THE AUTHOR

Harold W. Stubblefield has served as chaplain at Clover Bottom Hospital and School, Donelson, Tennessee, since 1960. He was pastor of Lamasco Baptist Church, Lamasco, Kentucky, for five years and was associate in the chaplains' department of Western State Hospital, Hopkinsville, Kentucky, prior to his chaplaincy at Clover Bottom.

A native of Kentucky, Mr. Stubblefield earned his B.A. degree from Murray State College and his B.D. and Th.M. from Southern Baptist Theological Seminary. His clinical internships were at Louisville General Hospital, Central State Hospital, Lakeland, Kentucky, and at Texas Medical Center, Houston.

This is Mr. Stubblefield's first book, but he is the author of several articles and has conducted conferences on "The Church and Mental Retardation".

DEWEY DECIMAL CLASSIFICATION NUMBER: 259

Library of Congress catalog card number: 65-10343

Printed in the United States of America

3.JE6413

25479

THE CHURCH'S MINISTRY IN

MENTAL RETAR- DATION

Harold W. Stubblefield

BROADMAN PRESS
Nashville, Tennessee

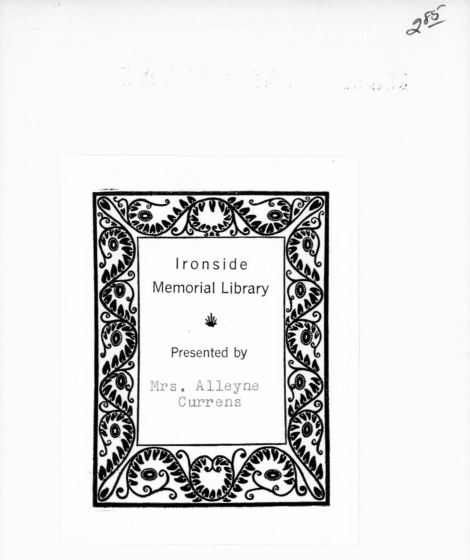

Ironside
Memorial Library

Presented by

Mrs. Alleyne
Currens

The Church's Ministry in Mental Retardation